"In *Unlimited Grac[e* ...]   [...]zing
grace of God. Many [...]   [...]race
personally. The church often struggles to apply the grace [...] [...]ately.
The unbelieving world desperately needs to hear the message of grace. In
light of these realities, I am thrilled to see this needed, Christ-centered, and
readable book. I wholeheartedly recommend it!"

> **Tony Merida,** Lead Pastor, Imago Dei Church, Raleigh,
> North Carolina; author, *Ordinary*

"Chapell unpacks how the entire Christian life, from beginning to end, is
by grace. The deepest message of the Bible and the ministry of Jesus Christ
is the extravagant grace of God to sinners and sufferers. This good news is
necessary to avoid the pitfalls of minimizing both the assurance of salvation
and sanctification. *Unlimited Grace* celebrates God's grace for all of life as it
addresses head-on the practical and honest questions about what this looks
like in real life."

> **Justin S. Holcomb,** Episcopal Priest; Professor of Christian
> Thought, Gordon-Conwell Theological Seminary; coauthor,
> *Rid of My Disgrace* and *Is It My Fault?*

"Bryan Chapell shows how God's love transforms us from the inside out. The
questions he recommends we bring to the biblical text (such as What does this
passage teach me about God the Redeemer?) are ones I recommend for teachers and leaders tasked with delivering God's Word on a regular basis. Let this
book remind you that the power of God's love is what moves us to obedience!"

> **Trevin Wax,** Managing Editor, The Gospel Project; author,
> *Gospel-Centered Teaching, Counterfeit Gospels,* and *Holy Subversion*

"When the prophet speaks for the Lord and proclaims, 'My ways are not
your ways,' we shake our heads in agreement while assuming that it can't
possibly be true. We assume that we know better, especially regarding the
things that will motivate God's people to desire to live holy lives. We assume
that the message of God's radical grace will make people into radical sinners.
That's because, as Bryan Chapell so wisely states, we don't understand the
'chemistry of the heart.' What makes the heart desire to love? What turns us
from ourselves outwardly toward our neighbor? Pastor Chapell has been a
gracious voice for years in my own life, and he really does understand that
heart chemistry. I'm so thankful for his faithful life and work and that I get
to recommend this book to you. I love it. I think you will too."

> **Elyse M. Fitzpatrick,** counselor; speaker; author, *Found in Him*

"Few books on the subject of God's grace are as balanced, practical, and clear as this one. Bryan Chapell's pastoral experience permeates these pages with both a realistic appraisal of the human heart and a compassionate, Christ-centered message of hope. This book is packed with insight into the mysteries of why we do what we do and how to live in the light of God's grace. Thank you, Bryan—I was helped."

Donald S. Whitney, Associate Professor of Biblical Spirituality, Senior Associate Dean of the School of Theology, The Southern Baptist Theological Seminary; author, *Spiritual Disciplines for the Christian Life*

"Once again my brother and friend has done what he does as well as anyone I know, or anyone in print. Bryan Chapell invites us to see and savor the endless riches and transforming implications of God's grace. There are so many reasons I'm excited about this book. At the top of the list is the invaluable wisdom Bryan offers to those who fear an overemphasis on God's grace. With the mind of a scholar and the heart of a pastor, Bryan shows us that we never balance grace with anything. Though it's certainly possible to misuse God's grace, it's impossible to make too much about what God has accomplished on our behalf through the life, death, and resurrection of Jesus. God's grace, and God's grace alone, gives us the motivation and means for living and loving to God's glory."

Scotty Smith, Teacher in Residence, West End Community Church, Nashville, Tennessee

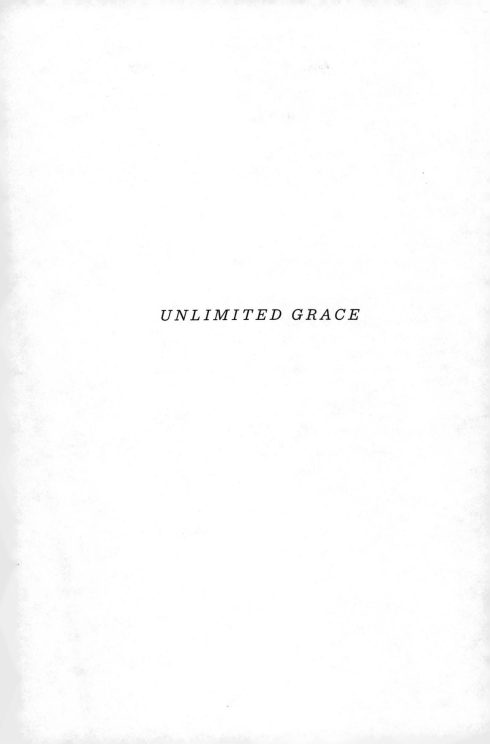

UNLIMITED GRACE

Other Crossway Books by Bryan Chapell

Holiness by Grace

Using Illustrations to Preach with Power

What Is the Gospel?

UNLIMITED GRACE

The Heart Chemistry That Frees from Sin
and Fuels the Christian Life

BRYAN CHAPELL

CROSSWAY®

WHEATON, ILLINOIS

Unlimited Grace: The Heart Chemistry That Frees from Sin and Fuels the Christian Life

Copyright © 2016 by Bryan Chapell

Published by Crossway
          1300 Crescent Street
          Wheaton, Illinois 60187

Cover design: Josh Dennis

First printing 2016

Printed in the United States of America

Scripture quotations are from the ESV® Bible (The Holy Bible, English Standard Version®), copyright © 2001 by Crossway, a publishing ministry of Good News Publishers. Used by permission. All rights reserved.

Trade paperback ISBN: 978-1-4335-5231-1
ePub ISBN: 978-1-4335-5234-2
PDF ISBN: 978-1-4335-5232-8
Mobipocket ISBN: 978-1-4335-5233-5

Library of Congress Cataloging-in-Publication Data

Names: Chapell, Bryan, author.
Title: Unlimited grace : the heart chemistry that frees from sin and fuels the Christian life / Bryan
    Chapell.
Description: Wheaton : Crossway, 2016. | Includes bibliographical references and index.
Identifiers: LCCN 2016015786 (print) | LCCN 2016031132 (ebook) | ISBN 9781433552311 (tp) |
    ISBN 9781433552342 (epub) | ISBN 9781433552328 (pdf) | ISBN 9781433552335 (mobi)
Subjects: LCSH: Grace (Theology)
Classification: LCC BT761.3 .C425 2016 (print) | LCC BT761.3 (ebook) | DDC 234—dc23
LC record available at https://lccn.loc.gov/2016015786

Crossway is a publishing ministry of Good News Publishers.

To Kathy,
through whom God's grace
fountains to multiple generations
and floods my heart

Contents

Part 3

ANSWERING HEART CHEMISTRY'S KEY QUESTIONS

Preface

No season of ministry has been more blessed than my years at Grace Presbyterian Church in Peoria, Illinois. I was invited to be the pastor of this historic church after three decades of teaching and administration at Covenant Theological Seminary in St. Louis. The church's offer that I could not refuse had three sweet attractions. First, the church was near family and friends. Second, the church offered the support of a wonderful executive pastor and managing director, who free me from administrative tasks and allow me to focus on the teaching and preaching ministries I love. Third, and most important, the leadership of the church asked me to help them minister the grace of the gospel that had transformed their own lives and vision for our church.

For many years, our church was a leading influence in our community. Much good was done, and many were helped as the church grew in stature and influence. But at some stage the growth stopped, stress fractures divided the congregation, and adult children walked away. The leaders could have blamed others, tested the latest church growth fad, or walked away themselves. They did none of these. Instead, they said, "We confess that we have grown proud, inward-facing, and self-oriented. We need help to learn to lead with humility so that we daily depend on the gospel ourselves and can really serve others in Christ's name. We want grace to be our identity, not just our title."

Those honest words of confession and hope, more than anything else, brought my wife, Kathy, and me to Grace Church. We thought, "This is the kind of leaders we need around us to understand the grace of the gospel better ourselves." And so we have been on a journey together with the dear people of our church to discern how the grace of the gospel can transform a church by freeing people from sin and fueling their lives with new hope and joy.

This book is an effort both to reflect what we have learned together and to teach the values that we hope will guide those who join us in this gospel endeavor. The phrase *Heart Chemistry* in the subtitle reflects what we know is a common concern about a ministry that focuses on the grace of the gospel. Many people will quickly do spiritual math and will reason that if all we teach is God's forgiveness of sin, then people will have no incentive to avoid evil.

We can always respond to such objections with the reminder of Jesus's words "If you love me, you will keep my commandments" (John 14:15). Our Savior knew there is a chemistry of the devoted heart that is stronger than the math of the divided mind. When we experience how great is his grace toward us, then our hearts unite with his. He changes our "want to" so that his priorities become our greatest joy, love, and compulsion. Through the blessings of grace, walking with Jesus is no longer a forced march of merit, gain, or protection, but a willing response of love, gratitude, and thanksgiving.

Part 1 of this book takes us on the journey to discover how grace not only frees us from the guilt and shame of sinful lives but also provides daily fuel for the joy that is the strength of Christian living.

Part 2 explains how preachers, teachers, counselors, mentors, parents, and all others who share God's Word can find grace in every portion of Scripture. My hope is that everyone will be able to see that grace is not a sidebar in the Bible but the consistent theme that culminates in the ministry and message of Jesus. Seeing grace in all of Scripture keeps us from segregating the Bible into passages that are about either being good or getting your due. Rather grace motivates and enables a life of loving God.

Part 3 attempts to answer the common questions people ask about how to find grace, and how to keep from abusing its blessings. I try to provide some plain answers while, at the same time, not ducking the hard questions.

Part 4 is not in this book; it is the chapter God is now writing on our hearts and in our churches as we seek to discover how far and deep and well the gospel of grace will take us into the heart of our Savior.

Part 1

HEART CHEMISTRY
FOR OUR LIVES

1

The King's Gift

Once upon a time, there was a king who looked from his palace window and saw one of his children collecting flowers in a distant field. The king watched as the child collected the flowers into a bouquet and wrapped it with a ribbon of royal colors. The king smiled because the ribbon indicated that the flowers were being collected as a gift for his own pleasure. Then the king noticed that the child—because he was a child—gathered not only flowers. From time to time, the child also added some weeds from the field, and some ivy from the border of the woods, and some thistle from the unmown banks of ditches.

To help his laboring child, the king gave a mission to his oldest son, who sat at his right hand. The king said to his eldest son, "Go to my garden and pick from the flowers that grow there. Then, when your sibling comes to my throne room with his gift, remove all that is unfit for my palace from his bouquet. Make it fit by putting in its place the flowers that I have grown."

The elder brother did exactly as his father had instructed. When the younger child came to the throne room, his brother

removed the weeds, the ivy, and the thistle, substituting all with
flowers from the king's garden. Then, the firstborn son rewrapped
the royal ribbon around the bouquet so that his sibling could present his gift to the king. With a beaming smile, the younger child
entered the throne room, presented the gift, and said, "Here, my
father, is a beautiful bouquet that I have prepared for you."[1] Only
later would he understand that his gift had been made acceptable
by the gracious provision of his father.

Grace for Weeds

This ancient parable sweetly reminds us of our heavenly Father's
grace. Each of us is the child with the weed-filled bouquet of good
works. Though we may strive with energy and zeal to honor God,
our deeds are never really worthy of his holy throne room. So our
eternal King graciously provides the holiness he requires. He has
sent his eternal Son, Jesus Christ, to make us and our efforts fit
for heaven.

Christ's sinless life, sacrificial death, and victorious resurrection are the perfect flowers that God prepared as substitutes for
our "weedy" works. As we rely upon Jesus's provision, rather than
on our own good works or intentions, he removes the flawed and
sinful deeds from the bouquet of our lives and replaces them with
his perfections. When we stand before God in his heavenly throne
room, everything we have given to God is made right by Christ's
work in our behalf. Christ's flowers are provided by the grace of
God that makes our lives' bouquets acceptable and pleasing to him.

The aim of this book is to identify not only how these truths
of grace affect our understanding of God's acceptance at the end

---

1. I have heard this adapted story variously attributed to Anselm, Francis of Assisi,
and Bernard of Clairvaux. I have been unable to find the source of the story in this form,
but it may be derivative of a passage in Bernard of Clairvaux, *On Loving God*, chap. 3; see
http://www.ccel.org/ccel/bernard/loving_god.v.html.

of our lives, but also how they empower our efforts to honor God every day of our lives. How grace makes our daily lives more like Christ's is not always obvious. After all, as precious as may be the grace that substitutes Christ's righteousness for our sin, and as comforting as it may be to know that God will provide the holiness he requires, such assurances may seem to let us off the hook for now.

If our works are not the basis of our standing before God, does that mean they don't really matter? And if God is ultimately going to credit us with Christ's righteousness, why should we bother to battle temptations or obey him?

The Math of the Mind

The answer to these questions requires us to acknowledge that there are some real, practical problems with the claim that God will substitute Christ's righteousness for our imperfections. There is a math of the calculating mind that figures, "If God will ultimately substitute Christ's good works for my bad behavior, then I might as well sin now." We don't have to sing, "Eat, drink, and be merry for tomorrow we die." We can instead chortle, "Eat, drink, and be merry for tomorrow God forgives." Any assurance of God's pardon has the danger of W. H. Auden's fictional King Herod's reasoning: "I like committing crimes. God likes forgiving crimes. The world is really admirably arranged."[2]

How do we answer that kind of logic? First, we should be careful not to counter this shady math by denying the gospel. Telling people that God will *not* forgive them later may scare some into temporary good conduct, but such a message betrays Christ. He taught, and gave his life to convey, the message that God would fully pardon all who trust that Jesus paid the final penalty for their

---

2. W. H. Auden, "For the Time Being: A Christmas Oratorio," in *The Collected Poetry of W. H. Auden* (New York: Random House, 1945), 459.

sin (John 3:16). God really will forgive those who truly trust him to pardon them. Whenever we humbly turn to God and ask for his grace, he will grant it.

You cannot claim as "Christian" any message denying that the grace of God is greater than all our sin and always available to cover it. New obedience and daily living in harmony with Christ's standards may enable us to *experience* God's forgiveness, but we never *earn* it. God is not waiting for us to get good enough to deserve his mercy and pardon. The Bible teaches that those who truly confess their need of God's mercy are truly forgiven (1 John 1:9). Though our sins be as scarlet marks against us, God will wash them white as snow (Isa. 1:18). He forgives murderers, adulterers, abusers, gossips, thieves, and liars (1 Tim. 1:8–16). He forgives us. No sin counts against us more than Christ's provision for us (Rom. 5:20; 1 Pet. 2:24). Christ takes the worst weeds from the bouquet of our lives and replaces them with fragrant flowers of God's eternal pardon.

The Chemistry of the Heart

So, if we cannot leverage good behavior by threatening that God will withhold his forgiveness from those who don't deserve it, how do we counter the manipulative math that is so ready to take wrong advantage of God's grace? We must employ a force stronger than raw logic—an impulse more motivating than calculations of personal advantage, pleasure, or gain. The force the Bible engages to motivate and enable us to serve Christ is the chemistry of the heart: love. Jesus said, "If you love me, you will keep my commandments" (John 14:15).

The apostle Paul echoes this when he says, "The love of Christ controls us . . ." (2 Cor. 5:14). Without sentimentalism or apology, our Savior and his messengers advocate a chemistry of grateful hearts that is stronger than the math of calculating minds. God's great grace toward us fosters such love for him that we want to please and honor him. His mercy toward us stirs such overwhelming thanksgiving in us that we desire to live for him. Love compels us.

How strong is this compulsion? Nothing is stronger. This is not simply a schmaltzy appeal to emotions. The most powerful human motivation is love. Guilt is not stronger. Fear is not stronger. Gain is not stronger. What drives a mother back into a burning building? Love for her children. Such love is stronger than self-protection, self-promotion, or self-preservation. Such love finds its highest satisfaction and greatest fulfillment in protecting, promoting, and preserving its object. A Christian for whom love of God is the highest priority is also the person most motivated and enabled to serve the purposes of God.

While there are many motivations that drive us—and many to which the Scriptures appeal—the foundation and priority of all that is done for God must be love for him, or else our expression of faith will inevitably be some form of dissatisfying selfishness. That is why Jesus taught that loving the Lord above all else is the foundation of our faithfulness to God (Matt. 22:37–38). Not only does such love enable us to find our deepest satisfaction in pleasing God; it also provides us the greatest strength for doing so. We will inevitably focus our resources of heart, soul, mind, and strength on what or whom we love the most.

The Power of Grace

What will spark such compelling love? That's easy. The Bible says, "We love because he first loved us" (1 John 4:19). God's greatest expression of love was giving his Son to pay the penalty for our sin. Through Jesus's sacrifice we are forgiven and freed of sin's ravages forever (John 15:13; 1 John 3:15). When we comprehend the greatness of this divine grace toward us, the chemistry of love stirs within us. And the more we perceive his grace, the stronger is our love.

Jesus taught that one who is forgiven much, loves much (Luke 7:47). Our love will be as strong as our realization of the guilt of sin and the hell of consequences from which we have been rescued. That is a primary reason Jesus and the apostles spent so much time warning people about hell. Their goal was not to scare us into heaven—that actually won't work, for reasons we will explore later. Their intention was to give us a soul-deep appreciation of the eternal rescue Christ provides. By his grace we are freed from slavery to passions and pursuits that leave us guilty, exhausted, and empty. As a result of our liberation, we long to embrace and honor our deliverer. His grace enables us to do both.

Heart chemistry ignites devotion that is more compelling and enabling than any mental math endlessly computing personal risk/ reward formulas. The priorities of a renewed heart trump the mind games that make sin acceptable even for a season. As grace ignites love for God, his priorities become our own. What most serves and honors him most satisfies and delights us. As a consequence, the apostle Paul claims with counterintuitive, head-spinning, life-changing confidence that the grace of God trains us "to renounce ungodliness and worldly passions, and to live self-controlled, upright, and godly lives in the present age" (Titus 2:12).

Heart Change

How can that be? If grace means our sins will be forgiven, how can it be a restraint on bad behavior? Isn't everyone going to figure, "Now that I got my grace ticket, sin city here I come!"? The answer is that grace draws the one to whom it is extended closer to the One expressing it.

Mercy and love magnetize the heart to Christ's priorities. The temptations don't depart, and the rules don't change in a grace-filled world, but desires do. The grace of God changes our "want to."

Prior to experiencing the grace of God, our inclinations are hostile or indifferent to him (Rom. 8:7). But when the kindness and mercy of God become profoundly real to us, at the same time that we deeply perceive how totally undeserving we are of them, then we desire nothing greater than to love him—and to love what and whom he loves.

I am not contending that grace removes all the allure of sin, but our love for it (which gives sin its power) is broken by the greater love grace produces. This dynamic signals the real power of change in the Christian life: we are ultimately controlled by whatever we love the most.

The alcoholic may hate the consequences of his addiction and intensely love his family, but at the time of intoxication the liquor means more. The workaholic may love her children with ardent devotion, yet love more the reward of a job, distancing her from them. An adulterer may tell his spouse with full sincerity, "She means nothing to me; I love you," but at the time of the unfaithfulness, the passion is loved more than the spouse. And the Christian who sins may say with complete honesty, "I love Jesus," but at the moment of surrender or rebellion, the sin is loved more than the Savior. An ultimate love ultimately controls.

Real change—real power over seemingly intractable patterns of sin and selfishness—comes when Christ becomes our preeminent love. When that happens, all that pleases and honors him becomes the source of our deepest pleasure, highest aim, and greatest effort. We honor him not merely out of duty and resolve—or to keep our distance from an angry God—but because our greatest delight is pleasing the One we love the most. The result is that the joy of the Lord becomes our strength (Neh. 8:10).

Chains of addiction, patterns of sin, and habits of apathy that have been forged by lesser loves are displaced by a surpassing love for the One who saves us from their power and consequences. When his delight is our greatest joy, we give our lives in fullest measure to his purposes.

With such ardor for Christ's priorities, Christians have suffered excruciating pain without losing their peace, surrendered possessions with undiminished passion for Jesus, endured family strife to maintain a testimony of his love, sung hymns to their torturers to display their Savior's heart, and turned from sin without regretting the cost.

No human math can account for these priorities. Yet, the heart completely understands such choices—and makes them. The following chapters are devoted to identifying how the truths of God's grace create this heart chemistry, changing the focus and forces of our life's pursuits.

2

Who and Do

Why is grace so important to the chemistry of the heart from which godly lives emerge?

To answer, we first have to understand what grace is. Grace is God's unmerited favor—"God's Riches At Christ's Expense," Phillips Brooks once said. Since God is entirely holy, we cannot earn his approval based upon our efforts. He's perfect; we're not (Rom. 3:23). In our sinful humanity, we constantly mess up, serve selfish interests, or fail to measure up to the standards of goodness that mark God's holy nature. So, to enable us to enter into a holy relationship with him, God provided his heavenly Son, Jesus, to pay the just penalty that these failures and shortcomings (which the Bible calls "sin") deserve.

Because Jesus was spiritually perfect, his sacrificial death on a cross fully countered the guilt of those counting on him to settle their problems with God. Jesus suffered for our sin, and we are credited with the result: our spiritual slate is wiped clean. We have the spiritual status Jesus did before he accepted the shame of our sins. That means we are holy in God's eyes. Jesus took our sin; we get his righteousness (2 Cor. 5:21). That's why grace is about getting God's richest blessings at Christ's expense. God provides for us what we could not provide for ourselves. That's the essence of grace.

Cleaning with Muddy Hands

Jesus deserved no punishment for sin. But, reflecting God's care, our Savior died on a cross, suffering for the sins of all who are willing to admit that they need his help. God doesn't force his care on people. If you don't think you need his help or don't want it, you are at liberty to reject his provision for your sins. But here's the problem: those who try to make themselves acceptable to God by their own efforts are comparable to someone trying to clean a white shirt with muddy hands.

Unholy people can't make themselves acceptable to a holy God. That's why God provides the grace of Jesus Christ. For us to be right with God, Jesus had to suffer the penalty our sin deserves. God didn't just eye the sins of the world and say, "Oh, that doesn't really matter; I'll just look the other way and let it pass." While that may seem gracious to a person whose crime is being ignored, the one who has suffered from the evil recognizes that it would not be gracious at all for God to ignore all sin.

Justice from a Gracious Heart

A person in our family once was assaulted in a terribly cruel way. When the criminal was arrested and tried, we did not think that it would be "nice" if the judge decided to do nothing. A world without justice is a world without grace; evil rules such a world. So how does God provide for justice and maintain his grace at the same time? He provided his Son to take the penalty that our sin deserved (Rom. 3:23–26).

God did *not* do nothing. First, he made sure that there was a just sentence dispensed for sin: Jesus suffered on the cross to receive the punishment that our sin deserved. But God didn't stop there. In order to be both just and gracious, he also declared that the penalty for sin didn't have to be paid twice. Christ's heavenly nature and perfect life made his sacrifice a sufficient penalty for all who want him to be their substitute. God doesn't require additional punishment once these scales of justice have been balanced (Rom. 6:10; Heb. 7:27; 10:12–18).

Paid in Full

Because he is just, there's no double jeopardy or double punishment with God. Once the penalty has been paid, it doesn't have to be paid again. And because he is gracious, God determined that all who confess that they need and want Jesus's punishment to serve as a substitute for their own will have no more penalty to pay—now or ever (Heb. 9:22–26).

What should be clear from this gracious provision is that freedom from the penalty of our sin is a result *not* of our merit but of God's mercy (Rom. 9:16; Gal. 2:16). He determined to be good to us before we could ever be good enough for him (Eph. 1:3–5). In fact, Christ was provided for us before we decided to accept his sacrifice in our behalf (1 Pet. 1:17–21; Rev. 13:8). So we should now acknowledge that we need him and trust in his provision, not in our being good enough to earn God's favor.

What happens if we ignore Christ's provision? Then we will face a judgment day on which people will have to explain why they didn't believe they needed Jesus. They will have to prove that they are as holy as God requires for an eternity with him. For all who have begun to *sense* their imperfections, and for those who *know* greater guilt, such a prospect is terrifying. But it need not terrify us anymore. If we acknowledge our need of Jesus, God mercifully promises freedom from the judgment due our sins and shortcomings—not because we earned our release, but because Jesus did.

The Internal Conversation That Misleads Us

Understanding this mercy, which is the foundation of God's grace, helps us answer the question that opened this chapter: "Why is grace so important to the chemistry of the heart from which godly lives emerge?" The answer now apparent is that grace not only promotes grateful devotion but also derails self-serving pride.

You automatically spark an internal dialogue in the minds of many people if you ask them, "Are you okay with God? Do you know that God loves you?" Their mental dialogue typically goes something like this: "Hmmm. Am I okay with God? Well, let's see. How am I doing? Was I a good enough person yesterday or today? Did I fulfill my responsibilities to others? Did I intentionally or unintentionally do anything wrong? Have I measured up?"

The question about whether a person is secure in God's love typically gets answered by consideration of one's own personal performance or competence. The previous discussion about the mercy of God should hint at why this internal dialogue is so off track. While everyone should be concerned about whether his or her behavior pleases God, the Bible makes it clear that our behavior does *not* determine his acceptance. His mercy does (Titus 3:4–5).

The Good Intentions That Pollute Us

The reason our good works or intentions are inadequate is not that there is no good in them, but that they are not sufficiently good. Our God is holy and requires holiness from his people

(1 Pet. 1:16). Holiness is about absolute purity. Whatever is holy has no hint of evil, bitterness, selfishness, pride, or disregard for others. We may do many things that have charitable and caring qualities but still fall short of God's holy standards. That is why the Old Testament prophet Isaiah said that our best works are like "polluted garments" (Isa. 64:6). That's not just an Old Testament perspective. Jesus also said that when we have done all that we should do, we are still unworthy of heaven's household (Luke 17:10). Being in God's family is not something we qualify for by our good deeds but a gift we receive by reliance on Christ's provision for us.

The Grace That Rescues Us

The apostle Paul emphasizes the inappropriateness of determining God's love by our behavior when he writes, "For by grace you have been saved through faith. And this is not your own doing; it is the gift of God, not a result of works, so that no one may boast" (Eph. 2:8–9). Our reception with God is a consequence of his grace, not of our works. Most Christians nod at this familiar truth, but fail to come to grips with its everyday implications.

Here's one of the most obvious implications: good behavior doesn't get you into heaven or out of hell. That's game changing for people banking on their goodness to get God's acceptance. But does that mean what we do doesn't matter to God? No. It means that good behavior has to be motivated by something other than a presumed payment or feared penalty for our performance.

Good deeds cannot be leveraged by promises to secure heaven or avoid hell through them. Our good deeds are simply not the basis of God's ultimate relationship with us. So it makes no sense to tell others to buy God's acceptance with their good works if we already know that no such currency works in his kingdom.

The Relationship That Motivates Us

But what else is there to motivate us to good deeds if our relationship with God cannot be purchased by them? The answer is *the relationship itself*.

Here's where the internal dialogue above went wrong: to answer the question, "Am I okay with God?" the person responded, "Well, let's see. How am *I* doing?" Whether the person was in a caring relationship with God was determined by how that person was "doing" in terms of meeting God's standards.

Who before Do

Such a person confuses our "who" and our "do." *Who* we are in loving relationship with God is not determined by what we *do*; rather, what we *do* is determined by *who* we are. That's why the apostle Paul encouraged believers in ancient Ephesus, "Be imitators of God, as beloved children" (Eph. 5:1). The command to imitate God (that is, to be holy as he is holy) is based on the family relationship with him that his grace already established. In essence Paul says, "Make *who you are* determine *what you do*"; he does *not* say, "Remember, *what you do* determines *who you are*" (see similarly Col. 3:12ff.).The identity God's grace establishes determines the behavior we imitate. Who we are establishes what we do—and *not the reverse!*

God's grace motivates our behavior; our behavior does not manufacture his grace. We live in *response* to his love, not to qualify for it or to make him produce it. Our obedience is a prayer of thanksgiving, not a bribe for blessings.

God fully purchased our redemption with Christ's blood. Our task is not now to live as though that were not enough, but to relish the opportunities to walk in the relationship he secured. Later chapters will explore this identity-obedience dynamic much more fully. For now, it is enough to understand that God's gracious claim on us is our greatest cause for serving him.

His grace does not detract from our devotion but fuels it.

Hearts before Flowers

One of my favorite church people is someone I met during the earliest years of my ministry. Maudette had been widowed many years, lived alone, and loved flowers. Though her advanced years kept her from tending her garden carefully, it provided a riot of colors and rare varieties that she loved arranging around the platform of our church.

Maudette came to our church only on Sunday evenings. She went to morning services at a church she had attended since she was a child—a church that had sadly drifted from its gospel moorings. Maudette stayed loyal to that church, hoping that her influence might help the succession of young preachers rediscover the gospel. But she came to our church in the evenings for what she called her "weekly dose of Bible."

The difference in the churches was never more evident than at Maudette's funeral. It was held in her childhood church. Her pastor said a few opening words, praising Maudette's many years of faithful Sunday school attendance. Then it was my turn to read from Scripture, and I read the passages she had chosen about the grace of God for all who trust in Christ.

Next her pastor gave the eulogy, assuring family and friends that Maudette was in heaven because she had attended church so often, was a sweet person, had a beautiful garden, and shared her flowers with the church.

Then I preached the sermon, as Maudette had requested, retelling the gospel truth that we are saved by grace through faith and not by works (Eph. 2:8–9). I loved rehearsing how Maudette's appreciation of her Savior's unconditional grace had kept her lovingly decorating his house for so many years—even after the stresses of age began to decay hers. But I wanted people to understand that the beauty was an expression of her love for Christ, not a payment or bribe to make him love her more.

My wife later said that attending that funeral was like watching two preachers boxing. One would throw a "goods works" left jab; then, the other would throw the "gospel" right cross. Who won? I don't know who won that day. I do know that Maudette wanted the gospel to win for the day her loved ones would face eternity.

Her hope was not in her flowers but in her Savior. She did not want who she was before God to rest on what she had done in her garden. Fragile flowers are beautiful, but our hope of eternity needs to rest on something far more firm. What we do must not determine who we are, but who we are by God's grace should determine what we do.

3

Order in the Court

If we confuse the *who-do* order, we will inevitably confuse our "justification" with our "sanctification." Those are big words with important meanings for Christians. It's good to get to know what they mean because misunderstanding them, or getting them backward, leaves people in perpetual insecurity, guilt, and resentment.

Made Right by Justification

Let's define the words first so we can figure out why their order is so important.

"Justification" describes what God does when he graciously pardons our sin to grant us the righteous status he requires for us to be in holy relationship with him. Since he sent Jesus to take the penalty for sin that we deserve, we are justified (i.e., made right) with God when we acknowledge that Jesus's suffering and death satisfied the penalty for our sin. Jesus took the condemnation that God could have justly imposed on us. When we depend on that mercy to make us right with God, he declares us blameless (i.e., justified) on the basis of Christ's provision (Rom. 10:9).

To understand justification, consider a courtroom scene where the judge declares the pardon of one whose penalty or fine has been paid. By assessing our debt fully paid by Christ, God justifies us, releasing us from any further judgment. And as our guilty status is removed, we become guiltless—a status that only the Son of God had prior to the provision of God's grace for those who rely on him (2 Cor. 5:21). Grace justifies guilty sinners so that they have Jesus's guiltless status before God.

Made Pure by Sanctification

Sanctification is about being holy as a consequence of being justified. Justification echoes the language of a courtroom to help us understand how Jesus's provision frees us from guilt. Sanctification echoes the language of the Old Testament temple to help us understand how Jesus's provision makes us pure, or holy.

In one sense, we are sanctified (i.e., made pure) at the very same moment that God justifies us. Since we have been pardoned by an act of God's grace, we are now holy to him. That is why the apostle Paul writes, "You were washed, you were sanctified, you were justified in the name of the Lord Jesus Christ and by the Spirit of our God" (1 Cor. 6:11). The apostle tells fellow believers that they "were sanctified" just as they "were justified" when the Holy Spirit enabled them to acknowledge their need of Christ. Already we have holy status before God because Jesus's work cleansed us from the taint of our sin. God's grace already and forever grants us holy and pure status in his presence (Rom. 12:1; Col. 1:22; 3:12). This spiritual reality can be called our "applied" sanctification—it's the purity applied to us.

Granted a Holy Status

Applied sanctification echoes aspects of Old Testament temple ceremonies in which unclean or impure things are purified for holy use. Though our sin pollutes us, we are sanctified by God's grace so that he can use us for his holy purposes. That's why the writer of Hebrews says, "We have been sanctified through the offering of the body of Jesus Christ once for all" (Heb. 10:10). God isn't waiting until some future day to consider us pure and precious to him.

We are already fit for his family and for his purposes because we are already sanctified by Christ's work in our behalf.

Designed for a Holy Purpose

Because our sanctification reflects ways in which things are made pure for holy use, we should understand that our pure *status* is not the only dimension of biblical sanctification. Sanctification is about being made pure for a *purpose*: to further holiness in us and others. God makes us pure for his use in the world about us.

Called to Holy Progress

This sanctifying use of our lives is a continuing and progressive process. The goal is still our holiness, but the process runs the full course of our lives as we grow in Christlikeness through ever-increasing understanding and honoring of God. We are given holy status to grow in holy service.

The writer of Hebrews connects the pure status God initially applies to his children with our continuing progress in personal holiness this way: "He has perfected for all time those who are being sanctified" (Heb. 10:14). God has already perfected our status (we are made pure by Christ's work), but that means God now expects us to act in accord with this status. The trouble is that we are not as perfect in behavior or intentions as we are in status. We are still "being sanctified." So there is still work for us to do in order to make progress in conforming our lives to the holy position God has already granted us by his grace.

This progress in personal holiness is probably what most people think about when they describe sanctification (whether or not they use that term). They are thinking about the expectation God has for our spiritual and behavioral improvement. These are good things. We expect our children to mature. We wouldn't expect God to want anything less for his children. But if we forget how our progressive sanctification relates to God's grace, our thinking can really take a wrong turn.

The Goodness Barometer

Because we know that God expects us to make progress in our sanctification—to grow in personal holiness—we can begin to think that our *status* is determined by our *progress*. We begin to base our justification (being okay with God) on our progress in sanctification (how *we* are doing with regard to personal holiness).

This line of thought basically leaves us evaluating whether God loves us based on whether we are being good enough to satisfy him. We make our goodness a barometer of God's care, measuring the degree of his love by the level of our devotion. As a result, we wonder whether our having a bad day is because we didn't satisfy God with a long enough "quiet time," or whether our child has leukemia because we didn't give enough money to our church, or whether hell is our destiny because we used it as a swear word.

Remembering Grace Is Grace

All the carefully constructed truths of the gospel collapse as a consequence of such reasoning. We must remember that our justification (being okay with God) and applied sanctification (being a pure child of God) are never determined by what we do but, rather, by faith in what Christ has done. God expects personal works of holiness as a loving response to his grace, but not as a way of gaining it. If we had to earn grace at any time in our Christian lives, it would not be grace.

Conditional Love Never Helps

To those concerned that removing obedience as a qualification for God's acceptance will encourage disobedience, we must again respond that the chemistry of a grateful heart is stronger than any rationalization of sin. The heart stirred by God's justifying and sanctifying grace will long to serve him.

In contrast, one who believes that God will love us only when we are good enough may serve him with vigor but will struggle, and almost inevitably fail to love him. The dynamics of spiritual affection are comparable to family relationships. A parent who promises to love only when a child's behavior measures up may get compliance (or rebellion or desperation) in response, but *not* love. Conditional love ordinarily creates resentment, destroying anyone's ability to honor Christ's foundational commandment: "You shall love the Lord your God with all your heart and with all your soul and with all your mind" (Matt. 22:37).

Further, if God's love is conditional upon sufficient obedience, then we have to ask, What actually qualifies as "sufficient" for a *holy* God—particularly when he has told us that our best works are as polluted garments to him (Isa. 64:6). If a twenty-minute quiet time is not enough, will a forty-minute one be "sufficient"? How much Bible reading, prayer, and church attendance will satisfy the condition, if doing all those things is the equivalent of throwing dirty clothes at heaven until God loves us? If the offering of Abraham's firstborn was not what God needed in Genesis, what sacrifice of mine will win God's acceptance now (Gen. 22:10–14)?

God Provides What God Requires

God answers the questions about the sufficiency of our obedience by offering his firstborn to make us right with him (John 3:16). He does not urge us to climb to heaven on our piles of good works. The gospel message from the earliest pages of Scripture urges us to trust that God will provide what he requires. Abraham's sacrifice of his firstborn would not have been enough. That is why God provided the sacrifice he required—a ram, prefiguring Christ, providentially caught in a thicket—and why Abraham called the place "The LORD will provide" (Gen. 22:14).

The religiosity that argues that we must earn or maintain the love of God by our holy striving actually dishonors the holiness of God (Ex. 15:11; 1 Sam. 2:2). His holy standards are as high as the heavens; his purity is beyond the hygiene of our best spiritual regimens. Pretending that our efforts meet his criteria diminishes him. Unless God provides the holiness that he requires, we have no chance of achieving it. Or, to return to the parable that began this book, unless God provides the flowers of his righteousness for the bouquets of our works, they are not holy enough for him.

Expressing Affection in Devotion

The good news is that God has provided the holiness that we need through the work of his Son (1 Pet. 2:24). Our job is not to repeat Christ's work but to honor it. We do so by trusting in the adequacy of his grace, and responding to it with lives of loving devotion. Such devotion—expressed in lives of service and praise to him—does not cause God to love us but is the evidence of our love for him. So, while grace destroys confidence in the adequacy of our efforts to earn God's love, it simultaneously stirs within us the desire to please him. Devotion to God results not as a means of qualifying for his affection but as a means of expressing ours (1 John 2:1–5).

Receiving Devotion with Divine Delight

I love repeating the story of a gift I prepared for my father during my early adolescence.

One morning, we were in the woods cutting logs to burn in our fireplace. We began sawing on a log that we did not know was rotten on the inside. So, when we had just barely sawn into the log, it broke and fell off the cutting frame. The log hit the ground so hard, that a big piece broke off. To my adolescent imagination that broken piece of rotten log looked like a horse's head.

My father's birthday came a few weeks later. So I took that piece of rotten timber, nailed a wooden board to it, tied on a rope tail, stuck on some sticks for legs, and partially hammered in a few nails (so they were left sticking out) down the length of the board. I put a decorative bow on my creation, and presented it to my father as his gift.

My father looked at what I had labored so hard to prepare for him and said, "That's wonderful!—What is it?"

I said, "It's a tie rack, Dad. See those nails sticking out on the side of that horse? You can hang your ties on them."

My father smiled, took my gift, leaned it against his closet wall (because the stick legs wouldn't really keep it standing up), and used it as his tie rack for years.

At the moment that I presented that rotten-timber-horsehead tie rack to my father, I could not have been more proud. I thought that my work of art was ready for museum display. But I had only to mature a few more years before my perspective changed. Then I said, "Dad, will you please get rid of that rotten piece of wood." But he received it and rejoiced in it, not because *it* was good, but because *he* was.

In the same way, God receives the "good" works that we offer him not because they are good enough, but because he is. As much as we may believe that our achievements deserve his honor, they remain defiled by our imperfections, weaknesses, and sin. Yet, God receives them, not because our works are pure enough for a holy God, but because he delights to receive the evidence of our love and to sanctify it by the mercy in his heart rather than by the merits of our craft.

Offering More Devotion to Delight Him

The sequel to my rotten-timber-tie-rack story is not difficult to anticipate. Because my father delighted in my gift—despite its imperfections—I wanted to bring him more. I did not worry so much that my gifts might not be all that they should be. Rather, I wanted to offer what I knew would please him. His mercy made my devotion a joy. And the desire to increase my joy and his made more and better gifts a foregone conclusion.

A Passion for His Purposes

Similar mercy from our heavenly Father sparks our devotion to him. Were we to believe that our works gained or secured his love, we would live under constant fear of his judgment. Our striving would be driven by uncertainty. We would be drained by dread. Our desire for his delight would likely be replaced by resentment of his pressure to perform or by our desperation to qualify for his approval. Thus, as counterintuitive as it may seem, the grace of God actually leads to a passion for his purposes. This is precisely what Jesus and his apostles said would happen. Jesus taught, "If you love me, you will keep my commandments" (John 14:15). Paul adds that the grace of God trains us "to live self-controlled, upright, and godly lives" (Titus 2:11–12).

Of course, where there is no sign of devotion, there is no evidence of real love for God or trust in his grace. And when the lapse of devotion results in God's discipline, there may be misunderstanding of his heart's desire to turn us from spiritual danger and into his embrace (Heb. 12:6–11). Thus, we are right to warn those who make no attempt to honor God that they may not presume upon his grace, and to warn those in rebellion that they may experience the discipline of a loving heavenly Father. But neither of these realities implies that our striving after holiness is the basis of God's love for us, or that our weaknesses drive him away.

When our waywardness distances our affections from him, we will find that whenever we turn back, he is always in our tracks with arms outstretched to receive us. His passion for us reignites and increases our devotion to him. We run to the arms that reach for us.

4

Care before Commands

How can it be that the holy God who requires our holiness does not reject his sin-soiled children? The answer lies in the reminder that we are made holy not by our efforts but by his. Before we ever make progress in our sanctification, he has justified and given holy status to all who trust in Christ.

The Obedience Throttle

For many years, I did not understand the constancy of God's care. I thought my level of obedience was the throttle on his heart—the more righteousness from me, the more care from him. Sometimes the Bible seemed to support this kind of thinking. I read passages such as this: "I appeal to you therefore, brothers, by the mercies of God, to present your bodies as a living sacrifice, holy and acceptable to God, which is your spiritual worship" (Rom. 12:1). But the way I understood it was like this: "I appeal to you therefore, brothers, by the mercies of God, to present your bodies as a living sacrifice *and then you will be* holy and acceptable to God, which is your spiritual worship."

I read "holy and acceptable" as though these words described a consequence of my presenting my body as a living sacrifice to God. In essence, I understood the verse this way: "You work really hard at being a good living sacrifice, and then you will be holy and acceptable to God." I made being holy and acceptable to God a result of my performance, that is, doing enough good stuff to be a "good" living sacrifice to God.

Yet, that is not what this verse or any other verse in the Bible teaches. The term "holy" should have been a clue. Never in my earthly existence will my performance meet the standards of God's unqualified holiness. I and all that I do will remain tainted by sin until I am in glory with Jesus (Rom. 3:23).

The Holiness Declaration

What I was missing was that "holy and acceptable" are not a description of what we will become; they are a declaration of what we are. We already are "holy and acceptable to God." But our minds reel with questions at such a claim. How can we already be "holy and acceptable" to God? We falter, fail, and sin. We are clearly not "holy," and truly wonder when we will ever be good enough even to be "acceptable."

The mystery is solved in the opening words of the verse: "I appeal to you therefore, brothers, *by the mercies of God.*" Our being "holy and acceptable" to God is a product not of our merits but of his mercies. He has sanctified us, washed our spiritual pollution away, and given us the pure status of his Son—not because we are holy, but because his mercy grants us Christ's status.

Identity before Imperatives

Following this verse in Paul's letter to the Romans are many imperatives, standards of holiness we are commanded to observe and to obey. The apostle lists individual, corporate, moral, and civil responsibilities that Christians should fulfill in order to honor God. But it is critical to note that Paul identifies *who we are* before he tells us *what to do*. He tells us that we are holy people before he tells us to do holy things.

Holy identity comes before holy imperatives. There are two reasons for this: first, it is impossible for those who are unholy to do holy things (remember that's like trying to clean a white shirt with muddy hands); and, second, the apostle wants us to remember that we do what God wants because of who he has made us—and not the reverse. He doesn't make us who we are because we have done what he wants.

The Old Testament Order

This order never varies in Scripture: imperatives are based on our identity. The word order may change, but the concepts never reverse. Even in the Old Testament, God did not say to his people, "You obey me, and then I will consider making you my people." Instead, he said, "Because I have made you my people, obey me."

For example, before God gave the Ten Commandments to Israel, he reminded his people, "I am the LORD your God, who brought you out of the land of Egypt, out of the house of slavery" (Ex. 20:2; Deut. 5:6). Then he commanded, "You shall have no other gods before me" (Ex. 20:3; Deut. 5:7), along with all the other commands.

First, God reminded the people of their identity: they were a free people because of his gracious deliverance. Only then did he give them his commands. He did *not* say, "You obey me, and then I will free you from slavery."

The imperatives that God gives in the Old Testament are always based on the identity he provides for his people. Obedience is always a response to God's grace, and not a way of gaining it.

The New Testament Order

When the apostles wrote their epistles to the early church, their letters also followed this order. First they wrote the doctrinal portions of the letter, explaining the ways that God's grace makes his people holy and his own (i.e., establishing their identity). Then, in the later portion of each letter, the writer would apply those truths to the way the people should live (i.e., establishing their imperatives). Again, the people's imperatives were about living consistently with the identity God's grace had already provided for them.

Present-Day Implications

We honor God's commands as a consequence of the grace that makes us God's beloved children. Our identity determines what we do; what we do does not determine our identity. The imperatives we honor are based on the identity we have, and the order is not reversible. The practical implications of this simple truth will change every relationship of those who determine to live in patterns consistent with the gospel.

The Way We Read Scripture

First, the identity-imperative order will change the way we read the Bible. No more will we open our Bibles and make our first task determining what duty or doctrine we must learn to make ourselves acceptable to God. We will, instead, rejoice to discern how God has made his people holy and able to obey him, so that his commands are the rails on which they can run to honor him—not to get to him. After all, the uniqueness of the Christian message is that God had to come to us in order to make us his own. Because we could not reach to him, he reached to us.

All other religions teach that in some way (by effort of body, mind, or will) humanity must reach to God. Christianity says that's not possible. God has to lift us to himself. That's why the story of the tower of Babel occurs so early in the Bible, telling all subsequent generations that trying to build your own "stairway to heaven" is *not* how you get to God (Genesis 11).

The Way We Teach Scripture

Next, the identity-imperative order will change the way we teach the Bible. No longer will we be tempted to say to any child, "If you are just a good little boy or girl, Jesus will love you." No matter how sweetly said or well-intended that message may be, we will recognize it as contrary to the gospel and a tool of Satan.

Jesus does not love any child (young or old) because the child is good. Jesus loves his children because *he* is good. While we were his enemies, Christ gave himself for us (Rom. 5:10). As sweet sounding as the words may seem about God loving us because we are good, and as effective as they may be for "guilting" children into good outward behavior, such words are spiritual poison. The message that Jesus loves us because we are good denies that the cross was either necessary or sufficient. The child who obeys Jesus to secure his love will be the adult who doubts Christ's love when life's temptations and challenges make it all too clear that we are not always his good little boys and girls.

The Way We Treat Children

How we treat our children will also change as the identity-imperative order begins to govern our words and actions. Before my wife, Kathy, and I understood how grace creates the heart chemistry of gospel motivation, we would discipline our children the way that we heard those around us. I would say to my son, "Colin, you are a bad boy because you disobeyed."

The words come so easily and are so common that I couldn't

hear what was wrong with them. The problem was that I was basing Colin's identity on what he did. He did a bad thing, so I said
that's who he was—a bad boy! But basing his identity on what he
did was not the gospel. The good news that Jesus came to share
with us is that our identity is determined not by how well we follow God's imperatives but by the relationship his grace provides.

So that my correction would echo the gospel principles that I
believe (and wanted Colin to believe), I had to change my words. I
began to say, "Colin, don't do that. You are my son, and I love you."
I wanted his actions to be based on his identity (the son I love),
not for his identity to be based on his actions. His actions would
vary; his family identity would not. He would always be my son,
and I wanted that reality to conform his heart to his father's ways.
I didn't want what he did to determine who he was; I wanted who
he was to determine what he did.

The Way We Treat Our Spouses

Gospel perspectives also changed the way Kathy and I treat each
other. I am enough of a North American male (shaped by the movie
images of John Wayne, Harrison Ford, and Johnny Depp) that,
when there are tensions in our marriage, I tend to react in one of
two ways: get mad or get uptight. And because preachers aren't
supposed to get mad, I tend to do the latter, expecting that she will
get the message through my silence.

Yet, as much as I may want to congratulate my self-control, my
aggressive quiet is no more consistent with the gospel than if I flew
off the handle. My silence is still designed to send a message, treat-
ing Kathy according to her actions. In effect, I base the character of
our relationship (who we are) on the failure I perceive in her (what
she has done). This, too, inverts the identity-imperatives order.

According to Scripture, we should consider our spouses as

"heirs with [us] of the grace of life" (1 Pet. 3:7). We are in a covenant of marriage that is supposed to be determined not by either party's immediate actions but by a prior commitment of each to a loving relationship. While there are certainly tensions and frustrations for us to work through, that work is to be done on the basis of the covenant we share, not the mistakes we make. Sure, there are still things to work through, but we do so based on the mutual love and respect we have covenanted to share, not based on wrongs we will inevitably commit.

The Way We Treat Others

The same principles apply to our relationships with others in our church. Our tendency is to treat them as they treat us. If they are nice to us, we are nice to them. And if they are mean to us, we either find ways to return the favor or ignore them. Yet, here again, we are defining people and our relationship with them on the basis of what they have done.

According to Scripture, our fellow brothers and sisters in Christ are members of his body. If we were able to look past the eyes that are angry or impatient with us, we would see Jesus indwelling those persons. Christ intends for us to relate to them on the basis of our eternal relationship with him—and them—not simply on the basis of their temporal tensions with us.

Again, I am not suggesting that such tensions are incidental or irrelevant. I am saying that those persons' identity in Christ trumps their behavior as we consider ways to reach them and rectify errors in them and/or ourselves.

The Gospel Contrast

The gospel pattern that prioritizes relationships over actions (i.e., identity over imperatives) as the primary motive for daily obedience is exceedingly difficult to maintain. The reason is that the lives of most people around us are geared to a performance-reward system.

If you meet or exceed expectations, performing well at work, then you are paid more and promoted higher. If you perform well in sports or music, you get the premier positions and greater acclaim. Many families function by offering or withholding affection based on how expectations are met—you are loved well if you do well. In all too many cases, what we do determines who we are in the estimation of others—and perhaps of ourselves.

The gospel short-circuits all such reasoning as the basis of our relationship with God and others. While God honors and treasures our obedience, it is not the reason he cares for us. His mercy, not our merits, make us his. The measure of our performance is not the barometer of his affection or our worth. Again, let's remind ourselves that our best works are only like a "polluted garment" to him (Isa. 64:6). This means that Christ must be the one who makes a way for us to our heavenly Father (John 14:6). Jesus's performance, not ours, determines our ultimate relationship with God (Heb. 7:25–27).

Our obedience does not determine who we are. His grace does. Out of love for God we should desire to honor his grace and not attempt to pay for it. Our good works show our love for him—they don't make him love us. His care precedes his commands and our attempts to meet them. But because he cares, we do. And that care will become the motivation and power of gospel living we will consider in coming chapters.

5

Family Trumps Failure

Imagine waking up one day, speaking to your spouse or roommate, and getting no response. No matter how loud and animated your words and gestures, your partner goes about the morning routines with no recognition of your attempts to get his or her attention. You might begin to wonder, "Have I passed on from this body? Am I dead?"

The apostle Paul did not wonder about such a predicament; he declared its reality for every Christian—even if our bodies are still alive. Because all our wrestling, striving, and working are not what make God love us, we might just as well be dead in terms of trying to make ourselves acceptable to God. Paul drove that idea home, saying that he was "crucified with Christ" (Gal. 2:20a). That sounds awful, but it's actually good news. It means that the "good" life of his own making, which couldn't justify Paul before a holy God, was not what counted in getting God's attention or affection. That life was as dead to God as Christ's lifeless body on the cross. In this way, Paul saw himself as united with Christ on the cross.

Paul was actually glad to be united to Christ in this way because it first meant that his past sins of persecuting the early church were not going to be counted against him. They were nailed to the cross of Christ, since Paul was identifying himself with Jesus there.

But not only were Paul's past crimes counted as dead to God; so were his "righteous" deeds. They would actually never be righteous enough for God's holy standards. Paul knew God's commands well enough to understand "that a person is not justified by works of the law" (Gal. 2:16). So Paul knew he had to depend on something other than his efforts to make him right with God.

The Works of Dead People

That "something" was someone: Jesus. Paul explains, "We also have believed in Christ Jesus, in order to be justified by faith in Christ and not by works of the law" (Gal. 2:16). Faith in the One who makes us right with God, rather than faith in our works, is the basis of our relationship with him. Our efforts are hidden behind Christ's—and that's good news, too, because the works of dead people are not going to get us very far with God.

In essence, Paul is reminding us that our destiny is tied entirely to Christ. Since the efforts of our lives are not why God accepts us, we are dependent upon Christ's sacrifice to reconcile us to God. In that way we are united to his death.

The Life of Christ's People

But that's not the end of the story. Paul adds, "The life I now live in the flesh I live by faith in the Son of God, who loved me and gave himself for me" (Gal. 2:20c). Jesus "gave himself" in sacrifice for our sin, so that we would live by faith in *his* work and not ours. But sacrifice did not end the story. Jesus rose from the dead. He is alive. Where does he live now? Paul says, "Christ . . . lives in me" (Gal. 2:20b).

The same Jesus, who conquered death and is interceding for us at God's right hand (Rom. 8:34) also now lives in us through the presence of the Holy Spirit, who represents him (John 14:16–20). So we are still spiritually united to Christ. There are two amazing consequences: new power and a new identity.

New Power

New power is ours because the same Spirit that raised Jesus from the dead now indwells us. The force of his spiritual victory courses through our mortal bodies, enabling us to perform God's purposes (Rom. 8:11). Christ's life in us grants us the ability to change past patterns and resist persistent sins. All things we now do for and through Christ change the course of our lives and also serve God's purposes, please him, and bless us.

New Identity

The greatest blessing of the indwelling Christ is our new identity. We are as good as dead in terms of being able to satisfy God by our human efforts. But Jesus is alive in us by his Holy Spirit. So we have his identity. His life, not ours, marks us before God—we're dead, but he's alive in us. His Spirit shines through and we are hidden behind his glory (Col. 3:3–4). This means that all the wisdom, holiness, and righteousness that Jesus possessed are credited to us—not because we achieved them, but because we are united to Christ who did.

New clothes. The apostle Paul explains, "You are in Christ Jesus, who became to us wisdom from God, righteousness and sanctification and redemption, so that, as it is written, 'Let the one who boasts, boast in the Lord'" (1 Cor. 1:30–31). Christ's characteristics are so identified with those of us in whom he dwells that it is as though his identity replaces ours before God.

We are clothed in his righteousness, hidden in his purity, indwelt by his Spirit, and enfolded in his redemption. Not only is he in us, but we are "in Christ Jesus"—endowed with his identity by the grace of God. Thus, we boast not about our goodness but about what our Lord does in and through us (John 14:20; Rom. 13:14; 1 Cor. 1:31).

New family. As we boast in him, he treasures us. Because we are united not only to Christ's death but also to his life, everything good associated with Jesus becomes part of our identity before God. God even calls us his children, granting Jesus's family status to us.

The apostle John writes, "See what kind of love the Father has given to us, that we should be called children of God; and so we are" (1 John 3:1). God loves *you* as much as he loves Jesus! Think of that! God knows all about our weaknesses, doubts, fears, and sins. Yet, he loves us no less than he does his own child (Rom. 8:29). I know that sounds impossible, but it's because our sinful self is dead before God and Christ now is our life (see Col. 3:4).

The Blessings of Christ's Family

Many special blessings are ours as a consequence of being united to Christ. Chief among them is the promise that God isn't waiting for us to measure up to some standard of perfection before loving us fully. Because the perfections of Christ's life determine our spiritual status, nothing in us spoils the love his Father has for us (John 14:20).

Unchanging Love

Because I am united to Christ, God's love for me is not as variable as my loyalty to him (Lam. 3:22–23; Ps. 25:6–7). God will not love me more because I do better. He will not love me less because I stumble. His love is based not on my behavior but on my union with his Son—a union built on trust in his grace, not my goodness.

Through that union, I have the identity of Christ and cannot be loved more, because I am already loved as infinitely as he. And because of that union, I will not be loved less, since Christ's life, not mine, is the basis of God's love. The heavenly Father loves me as much as he loves Jesus—and nothing will change that (Rom. 8:38–39).

Life-Changing Love

As my children have left for college, I have told each of them the story of my own departure from home. My father drove me to a school I had never visited, in a town I did not know. At first I was excited, but as our trip progressed, the magnitude of the change and risk involved began to overwhelm me. I stopped talking.

At some point, my silence spoke to my father, and he asked, "Are you scared?" I nodded yes. Then, he pulled the car off the highway, shifted to park, and turned to face me. "My son," he said, "I do not know what this school has in store for you. I don't know if you will do well or if you will do poorly. But you are my son, and nothing will ever change that. No matter what happens, there is a place in my home for you."

My father made it clear that being united to his family trumped any failure. That message encouraged, strengthened, and sustained me through many trials and troubles in my college years and beyond. And later in life, each time I told my own children that account, I also wanted the security of their family relationship to give them footing to face whatever fears or failures might come their way. That's the way our heavenly Father wants his assurance of our union with Christ to strengthen and sustain us. It's the way he wants us to encourage one another by echoing the assurance of these gospel truths.

Unfair Love

However, when my youngest daughter, Katy, went to college, she was determined not to let any fear or anxiety show that would necessitate such an assurance. The day we drove her to college, registered her for classes, and moved her "stuff" into her dorm room, she did nothing but chatter and smile.

Even as Mom and Dad were getting in the car to drive away, her face showed only sunshine. So, as I gave my final hug, I first held her at arms' length, looked her in the eye, and said, "Katy, I want you to remember what my father said to me. No matter what happens here, whether you do well or poorly, you are mine and nothing will change that. Our home will always be yours."

That did it. The smile vanished. Her face flushed. The bright eyes filled with tears, she hugged me hard, and she said, "Oh, Daddy, you know that's not fair."

Of course, it's not fair. It's grace.

6

Know the Path

I live in the "Land of Lincoln," that region of Illinois where Abraham Lincoln's political career sprouted. Here legend and facts about the great man so intertwine that it's hard to determine all that's true. But the tales of his life consistently reflect principles that drove him and still stir our hearts.

One such account relates that he gathered his meager earnings as a country lawyer and cast the highest bid for a slave at auction. Having purchased her, he immediately set her free.

Then she asked him, "Mr. Lincoln, are you really setting me free from these chains?"

"Yes," he said.

"Are you saying that I no longer have to follow a master?" she asked.

"Yes," he said. "You can go wherever you wish."

"Then," she said, "I want to go with you."

The Bondage of the Heart

True or not, the account rings with truths we well understand. Gratitude for release from slavery sparks loyalty for the one who provides freedom. Jesus taught the same when he urged those he set free from sin to abide in his Word (John 8:31–36). The apostle Paul even more explicitly says, "You who were once slaves of sin have become obedient from the heart to the standard of teaching to which you were committed" (Rom. 6:17).

Here is heart chemistry in biblical terms: freedom from slavery to sin sparks obedience of the heart to God's standards. We become committed to God's words and ways in heartfelt thanks for his mercy toward us.

The Need to Know

But the desire to show our loyalty and love for God creates a new problem. How can we follow God's standards if we don't know what they are?

Imagine a preacher who beautifully described how God gave his Son to pay the penalty for our sin and now calls all his children to honor Christ in loving response. The natural reaction in all who understood Christ's sacrifice and victory in their behalf would be to ask, "How do I honor him?"

Now imagine the same preacher answering with folded arms, a toss of the head, and a dismissive, "I'm not going to tell you." All who listened would be immediately distressed. "This is cruel!" they would say. "Why won't you tell us how to honor our Lord?"

If the preacher responded, "Because he won't love you more on the basis of the works that you do," then all would roll their eyes and say, "That's nuts!" The knowledge that obedience does not earn God's love doesn't remove a desire to honor him. When grace takes away concern to earn God's love, it does not erase a longing to express love to him.

We want to honor the One who has set us free from slavery to sin. But in order to be able to show our devotion to Christ, we have to know what honors him.

Knowledge Is Power

The power to obey our Lord requires that we know what honors him. Knowledge is power. We cannot do our Savior's will if we do not know what he wants. Teaching grace in such a way that God's people are left ignorant or insensitive to God's standards actually denies God's people their heart's desire.

The psalmist wrote,

Oh how I love your law!
It is my meditation all the day. (Ps. 119:97)

There could not be such delight in God's standards if meeting them were the basis of God's care for us. In that case, God could only be perceived as the frowning referee on the sidelines of our life. We would live in constant fear of him blowing some heavenly whistle and assigning penalties when we step out of bounds. And because we know that the only acceptable standard of obedience for a holy God is perfection, we would expect a lot of penalties. His law could only be something to dread, not delight in.

Knowledge Is Safety

The psalmist takes such delight in God's standards because they reveal the character and care of God. The principles of God's law establish a good and safe path for his people. God says, in effect, "If you stay on this path, you will find what is best for you in life, and you will be kept safe from spiritual danger." Such a path is *not* something we dread but is actually the guidance every believer seeks in life. What a blessing that God has already graciously prepared it for us!

As the safe and good path, God's law is a sweet provision for his people (Pss. 19:10; 119:103). The path does not earn us his grace but is an expression of it. So it would actually be ungracious (i.e., unkind and uncaring) to deny God's people knowledge of this good and safe path.

The Law of Love

The kind of teaching that puts God's law and his grace in opposition to one another doesn't actually understand how the Bible's heart chemistry works. While it is true that our obedience to God's law is not the basis of his love for us, that does *not* mean that God's standards are bad, irrelevant, or to be ignored. When my children were small, though my love for them was not because they stayed off the busy highway beside our house, I still expected them to stay behind our fence. God's standards reflect similar concern for our safety at every stage of life.

God loves us enough to say, in effect, "If you tell lies, people will not trust you," and "if you are not faithful to your spouse, you will destroy your family." These standards (and all the other commands of God) are expressions of love for those under his care. We keep and teach God's commands because he promises that his standards help us and honor him.

The Path of Blessing

We most fully experience God's blessings on the path of righteousness his Word describes. For most of us, most of the time, obeying God results in lives of relational warmth and material comfort (Matt. 6:30–34). However, this is not always the case, because these are not the only blessings God intends.

In this fallen world, everyone—even those who consistently obey God's commands—will experience a measure of suffering (2 Cor. 4:17–18; 1 Pet. 5:9). God's blessings cannot always be defined according to what most people in the world treasure. Not all faithful people have easy and carefree lives. In fact, Jesus promised his disciples that they would be persecuted (John 15:20).

The blessings of living for Christ always include being able to look in the mirror without shame and having cause for spiritual joy and peace despite our circumstances (Rom. 14:17). These are blessings the world can neither give nor deny. We can live without shame because Jesus took our guilt and gave us his identity. We live beyond the anxiety of present circumstances with the assurance that God works all things for good and promises an eternity of glory and peace in his presence (Rom. 8:18–21, 28). We trust this is so not because it is evident in our circumstances but because God has shown us his character at the cross (Rom. 8:32). We trust the path designed by the hand that gave us Jesus.

So we obey God, even when it seems to our personal disadvantage, because we believe that this is a moral universe and doing what God requires is ultimately best for us and others he loves. If no one were willing to live nobly and sacrificially for righteousness' sake, then all in the world would suffer without knowledge of the alternative life of spiritual peace and wholeness our Christ offers.

The Path of Pleasure

Even if there are no tangible benefits in this life, we obey God because his standards reflect his own righteous and holy character. By living for God in situations where there is no apparent gain for us, we demonstrate our devotion to him. We indicate that living for him is better than bowing to the pressures and priorities of the world. We honor what is honorable in him because nothing gives us more pleasure.

Living in accord with God's standards—no matter what else may challenge or tempt us—ultimately demonstrates that we believe that walking closely with our Savior is better than anything this world can offer. He is more lovely than anything else, and separating ourselves from anything that would distance or dishonor him brings us joy.

The Path of Peace

Obedience to God's standards is not a condition of his love for us, but it does affect our daily experience of his joy and peace. If we walk off his path of spiritual safety, we should not be surprised that there are consequences of our own making, or that God may express loving discipline as a means to get us back on the safe path.

Such discipline is never an indication of the absence of his love, but rather proof of it. Had he no love, he could simply let us wander off and face greater harm. So, even when we are in the throes of the harshest discipline heaven can bring, we are loved no less (Heb. 12:6–14). The divine hand that disciplines is simply turning us back to arms that embrace and protect us eternally. But whether trials are discipline or not, none of them undermines the love that acts to bring us ultimate peace and joy with God.

God's gracious intentions help us understand why healthy change in the Christian life requires knowledge of his standards. Apart from his commands we simply have no guidance for the lives of peace and joy that God intends.

Knowledge Alone Is Destructive

This context for God's commands also tells us why bare moral or doctrinal instruction is so often destructive to true Christian living. If all we do is teach people to be good or more doctrinally precise, they will inevitably think that their relationship with God is a consequence of their conduct or competence. It is not. Our eternal relationship with God is a consequence of trusting in Christ's death and resurrection—plus nothing.

As important as our conduct and competence are for fully enjoying our relationship with God, they do not establish or sustain his love. We do not become or remain God's children because of how good we are or how much we know.

I am not here contending that a wicked life and heretical doctrine are inconsequential to God. Persons who unrelentingly embrace either form of unbelief or wandering have scant personal assurance or experience of an eternal relationship with God— even when he keeps loving them (more on this in chap. 21). Still we need to be concerned about those who receive a steady diet of teaching about duty and doctrine without consistent reminders of God's love.

Duty and Doctrine Dangers

Duty and doctrine dispensed without grace can create only two possible human responses: pride and despair. If our most regular message to our children, fellow believers, or ourselves is "You should be better than you have been" or "You should refine your doctrine more than you have," then the result will not be progressive sanctification but progressive deterioration of spiritual health.

"Just be good" pride. Here's why. One response to a "Just be good" message is that of a rich young man who once met Jesus (Mark 10:17–22). The young man came up to Jesus on the road and said, "Good Teacher, what must I do to inherit eternal life?" (10:17). Jesus immediately understood the implications of the question "What must *I do* to inherit eternal life?" We don't "inherit" anything as a consequence of what we do. We inherit things as a consequence of our birth and what someone else has done. Similarly, we inherit eternal life only as a result of being "born again" through trusting in what Christ alone has done for us (John 3:3, 7, 16).

Sadly, the young man did not hear the irony in his question, so

Jesus stretched out the conversation. First, he echoed the young man's greeting: "Why do you call me 'good?' Only God is 'good'" (Mark 10:18, paraphrased). Then Jesus told what was required for the young man to be good enough for God: keep the commandments. In essence, Jesus said, "If your question is really what *you* must do to gain eternal life, then obey all the commandments."

The young man responded in precisely the wrong way. In answer to Christ's challenge to obey God's commands, the young man claimed, "All these I have kept since I was a boy" (10:20, paraphrased). Jesus had just said, "Only God is good." And what did the young man boast five seconds later? In essence, he declared, "I am good, too." He gave himself the status that Christ said God alone has. And in granting himself that status, the young man broke the first of the Ten Commandments (the one most important to the Jews): "You shall have no other gods" (Ex. 20:3).

Jesus was leading the young man down the path of humility, but the young man took the path of pride. Jesus showed that one potential human response to mere "Be good" messages is pride. Instead of being broken by the holy requirements of the law (i.e., be absolutely righteous in behavior, be exhaustively rigorous in discipline, be entirely right in doctrine), the person simply says, "I've done all that." And the implication is, "I really don't need God's grace to live as he requires."

The problem with claiming to have kept all the commandments, of course, is that God's Word teaches that no one is perfectly righteous or able to do all that God requires (Rom. 3:10). If we broke only one commandment, we would—in some measure—actually have broken all (James 2:10). They're all connected. Moral and doctrinal instruction apart from grace leads away from God—just as the young man who was so sure of his goodness ultimately walked away from Jesus (Mark 10:22).

"Just be good" despair. The only other possible response to sheer "Be good" messages is "I can't." That's despair. People assess the actual requirements of a holy God and simply give up. They rightly conclude, "I can't do all that God requires."

This attitude is initially reflected in the words of the Roman centurion who wanted Jesus to heal his servant. Despite the military officer's great power and position, he said to Jesus, "Lord, I am not worthy to have you come under my roof" (Matt. 8:8). He acknowledged that there was nothing in his life that deserved Jesus's help. He didn't have the goodness to qualify for Jesus's mercy.

But that's not the end of that story. Next the centurion said to Jesus, "But only say the word, and my servant will be healed" (Matt. 8:8). Instead of depending on his goodness or abilities, the centurion asked Jesus to take care of everything. In doing so, the soldier properly honored Christ above all other powers and privileges due a Roman officer. The centurion depended on Christ alone and, in doing so, honored Christ above all.

Dependence to Desire

That's what's supposed to happen. Dependence upon the grace of our God does not make honoring him superfluous. Rather, his great mercy makes our need to honor him our heart's desire. Knowing the requirements he gives to honor him provides much (but not all) of the power we need to satisfy that desire. That's why studying God's Word, learning from other believers, and listening to the prompting of the Holy Spirit in our hearts are so important for staying on the path God designs for lives of joy and peace. Simply knowing what blesses us and honors God is a sweet provision of God's grace.

Yet there is more we need to know, an even more powerful source of spiritual transformation, as we will see in the next chapter.

7

Know Thyself

Walking in God's ways requires knowledge of his good and safe path. But that's not all we need to make life changes that honor God and bless us. Having good directions does not guarantee that we will take them.

Bible teachers soon discover that most people already know what God requires most of the time. Hardly anyone is surprised that God commands honesty, kindness, purity, faithfulness, and so forth. Still, people choose different paths.

So is growth in godliness all about applying tons of grit and determination to stay on the path we know? While we certainly need to exercise our will, that will not be enough either. Fatigue, error, distraction, or the appeal of other paths can derail the strongest determination. Cloudless days that boost our resolve to stay on God's sunlit path are not endless.

Know You're Human

Knowing ourselves—our strengths, weaknesses, inclinations, susceptibilities—is also necessary to walk the path God has designed to bless our lives. The first thing we need to know about ourselves is that we are human. I know that seems obvious, but without facing the implications of being human, we will be unprepared for the challenges of staying on God's path.

You're Vulnerable

The first implication of being human is that we are vulnerable to temptation. We may think that our character, background, training, or resolve would make us impervious to the assaults of Satan that others experience, but that would be a grave error.

Immature teenagers may act as if they believe they are immortal, invincible, and infertile, but mature believers should not be so naïve. The apostle Paul writes, "No temptation has overtaken you that is not common to man" (1 Cor. 10:13). We are all temptable. This is the common plight of all humans. By nature we are all vulnerable. We share struggles with sin.

Early in my Christian life, I was comforted by this idea of shared struggle. I thought it meant that there was no temptation I experienced that people somewhere in the world did not also experience. I was glad to know I wasn't alone. That comfort is still a blessing, but I no longer have such a limited view. Now I understand that the apostle means there is no struggle in others' hearts that I do not share in some dimension or degree. There is no jealousy, no lust, no anger, no greed, no sin whose seeds are not also in me—in us all.

If that sounds unlikely, we should remember (as mentioned previously) that the Bible tells us that when we have broken one of God's commands, we have actually transgressed them all (James 2:10). Each command represents a dimension of faithfulness to God, and when we break one, our disloyalty spills over to the other dimensions. For example, if we steal, we at the same moment take in vain the name of the God we represent, are faithless to him, bow to the god of greed, covet another's possessions, and so forth. Breaking just one commandment causes us to share aspects of sin that are common in all of humanity. So Paul writes, "All have sinned and fall short of the glory of God" (Rom. 3:23).

I stress the susceptibility that all humans have to temptation because if we do not recognize our personal vulnerability, then we are in grave spiritual danger. Not knowing that we are nearing the cliff's edge of temptation, or that our adversary is crouching at our door (Gen. 4:7; 1 Pet. 5:8), makes us easy prey. Acknowledging our vulnerability should stir us to take proper precautions. God graciously provides them because he also knows we are human.

You're Teachable

God's precautions often come as practical advice that will keep us on his path of blessing. For example, parents, teachers, and youth leaders help children avoid dangerous peer pressure by sharing God's warning that "bad company ruins good morals" (1 Cor. 15:33). The principles of grace do not negate the importance of telling others what they should know in order to avoid temptations. Withholding practical instructions that help steer others from moral pitfalls and heartache is not gracious. God makes us teachable for a reason. Because we are human, we need practical instructions that help us steer clear of dangerous temptations or get us out of their tar pits.

If we know someone who is struggling with addictive behaviors or relationships, we really do help them by sharing practical advice. For example, we advise, "Don't take that route home from work because, if you do, you will get too close to the place or person that tempts you." This is not arbitrary legalism. Such instruction echoes the Bible's practical instruction:

> Do not enter the path of the wicked,
> and do not walk in the way of the evil.

Avoid it; do not go on it;
    turn away from it and pass on. (Prov. 4:14–15)

Such behavior modification is often effective, and has even been adopted by secular psychologists, because there are common aspects of our humanity that make such practical instruction helpful. But while such practical advice is biblical and necessary, it does not exhaust our arsenal of spiritual weapons. We have not yet begun to discuss the heavy weapons of grace that operate beyond our common humanity. That's why the practical advice of Dr. Phil, Oprah, or Ellen is no substitute—or match—for the instruction of a prophet like Jeremiah or an apostle like John.

Know You're Redeemed

What do the biblical authors tell us that the secular advisors do not? Prophets and apostles speak to believers not only as those who are human but also as those who are redeemed. We are not properly prepared to progress in Christlikeness until we also know the powerful benefits of this provision of God's grace.

Loved by the Father

In the first five chapters of this book, we considered the new status that we have as we put our trust in Christ. Because he paid the penalty for our sins and shares his righteous identity with us, the heavenly Father loves us as much as he loves Jesus. We don't earn or deserve this love. It is not based on what we do. Consequently, God's love does not wax and wane with the rising and falling tides of our attitudes or behaviors.

When we know that God's love for us is not as fragile as our resolve, our love for him grows. That love stimulates a greater willingness to serve him, stirring courage to risk ourselves for him and creating longing to return to him when we have wandered

(Rom. 2:4). Divine arms always outstretched toward us strengthen us for our spiritual battles and beckon us toward recuperation and renewal when we have fallen.

United to the Son

Not only are we loved by the Father; we are also united to his Son. By this union we share Christ's identity, position, destiny, *and* power.

As already discussed, we have Christ's identity because (1) he has taken the penalty for our sin, granting us the holy status that he alone possessed, and (2) all human defects that marred our identity have been covered by Christ. Since our pasts are dead to God (Gal. 2:20) and our lives are hidden in Christ (Col. 3:3), our God regards us with Christ's infinite and unchangeable righteousness. Our spiritual bank accounts are filled with his goodness. We are so secure in God's heart that he has already granted us heavenly status (Eph. 2:6). God delights in us because Jesus has united us to himself, making us members of his body (1 Cor. 12:12–27), instruments of his glory (Rom. 6:13), and sharers of his destiny (Rom. 8:17–18).

Indwelt by the Spirit

Because we share Christ's identity, we have his privileged position at God's right hand (Eph. 2:6; Col. 3:1) and we are also assured of eternity with him (Col. 3:4; 1 Thess. 4:17). But we do not have to wait for our entry into heaven to begin enjoying the benefits of our union with Christ. He *already* indwells us and, by the Holy Spirit of knowledge and power, *now* enables us to live for him (John 14:16–20; 1 Thess. 4:8). We face great spiritual challenges, but Christ sent the Holy Spirit into our hearts to grant us the wisdom and strength to honor him (John 14:26; 1 Cor. 2:14; Eph. 6:10).

Know You're a New Creation

Knowledge of these already-mentioned aspects of our redemption is vital if we hope to see change in our spiritual lives. When Paul adds up what it means for us to be loved by the Father, united to Christ, and indwelt by the Spirit, the apostle concludes that we are "a new creation" (2 Cor. 5:17). As a consequence, Paul says that we are now able to be "ambassadors for Christ, God making his appeal through us" (2 Cor. 5:20).

It all *sounds* so nice—we have been made new so that we can represent Christ. But all of us immediately recognize the problem with such a claim. We don't *feel* like new creatures. We still sin, doubt, and struggle. We still fit in the same bodies, have the same faces, and wrestle with many of the issues that we had prior to faith in Christ. So in what way are we new creations?

A Changed Nature

Being a new creation does not mean that we suddenly have the body of a model, the mind of a prophet, or the DNA of an apostle. Paul is not talking about physical changes, but rather a fundamental change in our spiritual nature.

Here's what's different. Before we were united to Christ, we were *not* able *not* to sin (Rom. 8:7–8). I am not saying that we were only able to commit crimes. But I am saying that our lives were not at all directed toward honoring and pleasing God. Self-interests dominated our thoughts and efforts (1 Cor. 2:14).

For those of us in relatively stable and cultured situations, life was spent pursuing expectations that preserved our social status and familial acceptance. For those in survival mode, looking out for number one may have led to painting outside the lines of polite society. But in either case, what ruled us was what most advantaged us apart from considerations of loving and honoring God.

A Changed Ability

What's different for those who are united to Christ? We are no longer controlled by ungodly priorities. We have the ability to resist sin and pursue God's priorities. I am not saying that suddenly we've become perfect in conduct. I am saying that we have a whole new life orientation. As the Holy Spirit reveals sin and selfishness to us, we are able to confess and address the wrong. Because the same Spirit that raised Jesus from the dead now indwells us, we have Christ's power to aid our resolve and conquer our sin.

Because we are new creations, spiritual change is possible in our lives. Tomorrow doesn't have to be like yesterday. We can make real progress against sin patterns, persistent weaknesses, and compelling temptations. That's the greatest blessing of having Christ living in us (Gal. 2:20). We have his power as well as his identity. Our new nature is not in name only; we are new creatures in spiritual ability.

New Perspective

It is necessary for us to know this truth about our changed nature because, if you do not believe that spiritual change is possible, you will not strive for it. Knowing we can change keeps our hearts engaged and our hopes alive. In contrast, if we do not believe that spiritual victory is attainable, we have already lost the battle. That is why the apostle John assures each of us, "He who is in you is greater than he who is in the world" (1 John 4:4).

Through our doubts and the accusations of our conscience, Satan comes to us and whispers, "You cannot correct this sin. You cannot help it. You have struggled with this for so long, it's now a part of you. It's just the way God made you. He's actually the one to blame." The biblical response to each of those claims is, "That's a lie! The risen Lord Jesus indwells me by his Holy Spirit. Greater is he that is in me than he that is in the world. I am not under the control of sin. I am not enslaved to my past or my passions. I am a new creation in Christ Jesus."

New Power

The apostle Paul exults in the power that is now ours as a benefit of our union with Christ. Says the apostle, "We know that our old self was crucified with him in order that the body of sin might be brought to nothing, so that we would no longer be enslaved to sin" (Rom. 6:6).

We are no longer slaves to sin. "Sin will have no dominion over you," Paul rejoices, because "you have been set free from sin" (Rom. 6:14, 22). Compulsions do not have control of us. Pasts do not predetermine the future. Backgrounds do not block hope. The Bible's assurance that a believer is a new creation is Christ's promise of a new life, a life free from bondage to sin.

Knowledge of who we really are as new creations in Christ Jesus enables us to live new lives free from sin's control. Such knowledge gives us power to confront the lies of Satan, to quiet the doubts of our hearts, and to act in accord with the promise of Scripture "I can do all things through him who strengthens me" (Phil. 4:13).

Christ's power is ours. We experience the amazing control it grants through the heart chemistry described in the next chapter.

8

Love Controls

Now we come to the most critical question in this book: If grace grants us Christ's status *and* power, why do we still sin? The Bible clearly tells us that temptations are not more powerful than God's provision. God always makes a way of escape (1 Cor. 10:13). Beyond that, he promises that our backgrounds and passions do not rule us. We are new creations. Sin no longer controls us. His Word assures us that sin shall have no more dominion over those whose faith is in Jesus (Rom. 6:6, 14, 22).

We are no longer slaves to sin. So why do we sin?

The Truth We Hate

As distasteful as the truth may be, the answer to "Why do we sin?" is "Because we love it." We sin because we love it. Consider this: if sin did not attract us, it would have absolutely no power over us. We yield to sin because we find it attractive, beneficial, pleasurable, or advantageous (John 3:19; James 1:13–14). Our compulsions, not sin's power, put it in the driver's seat. Sin's fuel resides in our affections.

A sensitive conscience may react, "No, I love Jesus. I confess that I sin, but I still love Jesus." That may be true, but in the moment of the wrongdoing, the sin is loved more. We sin not because we don't love Christ at all but because we don't love him above all.

As mentioned earlier, our sins cause us to say to Jesus the sad words of an unfaithful spouse, "My dear, I love you. That other pursuit meant nothing to me." The first words are true. The spouse at home is and was loved. But the last words are the lie. At the time of the sin, the other person or the passion is loved more.

Sin gains power over us not by its indomitable force but by our divided heart (Rom. 6:12; Gal. 5:24).

The Truth to Love

So, if our love of a sin is what grants the sin power over us, how do we get rid of that love? The scriptural answer is plain: with a greater love.

John Owen's classic book *The Mortification of Sin* (i.e., killing sin's power) teaches that we overcome the power of anything by shutting off its life source. Since the life source of sin is our love for it, we defeat sin when we deprive it of our affection—or displace it with a greater affection.

Filling with Love

For many years, our family has loved vacations at a cabin in the woods. We love the cabin in every season, but as winter approaches, we must drain water out of all plumbing systems, lest freezing water burst pipes. We shut off the water main and open all the drain valves. We reverse the process in springtime, closing drain valves to let the water fill the systems.

The hot-water tank requires a different process. As we refill the tank, we open a valve at its top, allowing inflowing water to drive out the air that occupied the space during the winter. In a similar way, when the love of Christ fills our heart, we drive out the air in which sin has thrived when our hearts have been cold to him. Love for Christ displaces love for sin and denies it the spiritual oxygen it requires to occupy our hearts.

Filling with Power

When our love for Christ is preeminent (first above all things), it drives out love for sin and spurs our devotion to him (Col. 1:18). The nineteenth-century Scottish preacher Thomas Chalmers described this process as "the expulsive power of a new affection."[1] Our behaviors change as our affections change. We conquer sinful passions not by constant Herculean efforts of the will but by actually seeking to act in accord with our changed desires (Rom. 8:5–6). I am not saying that battling sin never requires intense, exhausting spiritual warfare; I am saying that lasting peace and power require and result from changed affections.

The Love That Controls

Invariably, our life's energies and efforts are controlled by what we love the most. That is why the apostle Paul wrote of believers, "The love of Christ controls us" (2 Cor. 5:14). Not only does Christ control our eternal destinies by securing our souls; he also grants power over our present deeds and decisions by securing our hearts to his. Jesus similarly said, "If you love me, you will keep my commandments" (John 14:15). He was not simply chiding his disciples to test their love by their loyalty. He was affirming the consequence of our love for him. When he is our first love, walking with him is our first priority.

---

1. Thomas Chalmers, *Sermons and Discourses*, 2 vols. (New York: Carter, 1844), 2:271.

Walking in Love

I began ministry as a young man driving from seminary to preach at a little country church on the weekends. One Sunday, an elder asked if I would like to go with his family on a picnic after the service. I was single, and free food was being offered—I quickly agreed. The sunny fall day made the trip stunningly beautiful. We drove a scenic river drive to a restored Victorian village in the midst of a forest made golden and scarlet by fall leaves in royal display. Then, after the picnic, the twenty-something daughter of the elder asked if I would like to take a walk with her. I still remember how her blond hair shone and her green eyes sparkled in the radiance of the day. And I remember answering, "I'd love to take a walk with you!"

Of course I wanted to walk with her. She was beautiful, and as my heart filled with love for her, I wanted to walk all the more closely to that beauty—and have now for more than four decades.

So also, as our understanding of the beauty of God's grace fills our hearts with love for Christ, we want to walk with him. Love for him changes our desires and his priorities become ours.

Walking with Power

It bears repeating that the priorities of love are the most powerful human motivation.

Those who write or speak a lot about the grace and love of God are sometimes accused of dousing every message in lovey-dovey sentiment that has no power for life's real challenges. Grace can be misrepresented. But the sentimentality of some should not blind us to the solid fact all can witness: love is life's greatest power. Love—whether of country, family, or faith—has driven the most powerful movements of human history and points us to the most powerful motivation in human existence.

No motivation is stronger than love. Guilt is not stronger. Fear is not stronger. Personal gain is not stronger. While each of these can motivate people for both good and evil, none is stronger than love. Though the Bible uses many motivations to help secure our obedience, one command exceeds all others: love for God, which motivates lives that honor him and bless those he loves (Matt. 22:37). The plurality of motivations in Scripture should not blind us to its priority: love comes first! Why? Because love controls us (2 Cor. 5:14).

The Source of Love

The natural quest for those who know the power of love is to seek its source. Where does the love come from that captivates and compels the heart? The Bible answers, "We love because he first loved us" (1 John 4:19). Our hearts respond in love to love.

Unchanging Love

The reason that the message of God's gracious nature is so consistent (and necessary) in Scripture's instruction is that an understanding of heaven's heart captivates ours. Grace unfolds on every page: God's long march through the history of human rebellion and ruin to reach us with the love of his Son; the Savior's humble service, sinless life, sacrificial death, victorious resurrection, and promised return; the Holy Spirit's indwelling witness, power, and advocacy—all unswerving despite our wayward ways and hard hearts. These multiple dimensions of grace, and ten thousand more in the pages of God's Word, express God's love to garner ours. This is also why later chapters of this book focus on understanding how the beauty of God's grace unfolds throughout the Bible.

Grace Chemistry

Grace is the catalyst of the heart chemistry of faith. Through grace we experience the love that ignites ours. So, even though some people think of grace as granting license to sin, the apostle Paul comes from the opposite direction, saying, "For the grace of God has appeared, bringing salvation for all people, training us to renounce ungodliness and worldly passions, and to live self-controlled, upright, and godly lives in the present age" (Titus 2:11–12).

Isn't that strange, or at least counterintuitive? Instead of releasing us from all godly pursuits, grace trains us in them. Here again is heart chemistry trumping manipulative math. While the wandering mind searches for excuses, exceptions, and escape clauses, the wooed heart longs to show love in ever-greater expressions of devotion. When the renewed heart controls, the mind works to discover how to love God better, not how to abuse his grace.

9

Bread, Not Bribes

Because the love that grace generates controls believers, it empowers as well as motivates obedience. This insight is important because we may have the impression that teaching grace is all about providing proper motivation. It's more than that. Grace not only provides us reason to follow Christ, but it also provides needed power—not only motivation but also enabling. We need both because discovering *how* we change becomes crucial for the heart longing to do so.

The Desire to Change

Early in my ministry, my counsel was sought by a young man struggling with alcohol. He came regularly to my office and talked earnestly in our conversations. My office window was on a corner of the building, angled toward the front entry. So I could see my counselee approach the building, hide his beer behind a column on the porch, and then come into my office for counseling. He talked about wanting to stop. I don't believe he was lying. I think he desperately wanted to be free of his addiction. But it obviously had control of him.

My approach to counseling, at that time, had most of the features it presently does. We talked about the consequences of his addiction, the path it had followed when its pressures were most intense, the standards of Scripture, the sin patterns that sustained the addiction, the power of prayer, and the need for genuine repentance, as well as avoidance and accountability measures. All of these are good and necessary features of biblical counseling. But none was his final answer.

Even today I still have no silver bullet. But as I evaluated the conversations we had, the subjects we covered, and the measures we took, I began to recognize a significant gap in my approach. In fact, my friend's long-term wrestling with addiction marked a question I struggled to answer for many years. My question was not whether my counseling measures were biblical or necessary. I believed then and still believe they were. Though I do not consider myself a counseling expert, I think I can recognize approaches that respect biblical truth, reflect the observations of counseling sciences that are consistent with Scripture, and are applied by wise and caring practitioners. But my question was Why do these measures help some and not others? Why were my own efforts so inconsistent? What was I missing?

The Question of Change

My question boiled down to trying to understand why some persons change and others do not. I especially wanted to discern what made believers change so that I could apply that to my counseling, advising, and preaching.

I did not find much help among my peers in the helping professions. Except for the bizarre practitioners, most of those who claim to be guided by Scripture followed methods very similar to my own. Some gave greater emphasis to prayer, or meditation, or Scripture memory, or journaling, or accountability partners, or background analysis, or some other feature of solid counseling. But their tool kits all had fairly recognizable equipment, applied in varying ways according to the training of the counselor or the specifics of the situation.

I recognized, as I considered these various approaches, that they all basically fell under the what-to-do-about-it category of counseling. The counselee would tell the counselor what was troubling, and the counselor would give insight into the problem and then tell the counselee "what to do" to get healthy. That's what counselees want, and it's what we expect will promote spiritual change. We take similar approaches in preaching, teaching, parenting, and so on. And as this approach is exercised with appropriate knowledge and care, people make progress in their struggles—so long as they are properly motivated.

The Motivation of Change

I recognized in my counseling, long before I did in my preaching, the power of a proper love to motivate healthy change. I saw the need for such motivation because I rarely found myself telling people anything they did not already know they should do or had not already considered doing. While wise structures and practical steps were helpful for steering them from sinful and destructive behaviors, few people expressed surprise about the directions I gave. Despite thousands of excuses and rationalizations, hardly anyone said, "I never before thought that lying [or temper outbursts, or abuse, or being intoxicated, or cheating on my spouse] was wrong."

Few people excused their addictions, were honestly confused about their wrongdoing, or were proud of their sin. Virtually everyone already knew what was right and what was wrong. Most of the time, what they needed more than some biblical proof of their wrongdoing was sufficient motivation to take positive steps to change.

But even this was not enough. People would say, "Pastor, I dearly want to change. This struggle in my life is destroying me and those that I love. How can I change?"

The *How* of Change

That was the question that stumped me: How? For years, I thought the *how* question could be answered by greater diligence in the biblical disciplines (pray more, read your Bible more, go to church more, follow accountability measures). But I ultimately came to recognize that these could be understood as more what-to-do measures. Something was still missing.

Not Disciplines Alone

The disciplines were helpful, important, and necessary but could easily be interpreted as greater expressions of human will and diligence. For many people, setting up discipline systems and accountability measures was just another flavor of "try harder." The implicit message was, "It's all up to you. As long as you exercise appropriate willpower, discipline, rigor, and faith, then you will make progress."

Not Willpower Alone

I observed that the progress people made through all these means was often for a different reason than they or their counselors recognized. Many strugglers believed they were making progress because *they* were putting in the work and diligently practicing their disciplines. They often relied on willpower that lasted for a time but then lapsed. They discovered that personal resolve can be very powerful but needs extraordinary fuel.

Not Consequences Alone

Others were genuinely helped by the new patterns of life the disciplines encouraged, and by remorse for their past sin. For these people, facing the consequences of their sin was profound and course altering. They did not want to return to the life of their shame, pain, and struggle. Dread of return to the past sustained their disciplined pursuit of a better future.

The experience of those who found motivation in a better life began to shine a light on the answers I was seeking. I realized that the persons motivated by remorse had made progress (even if it initially involved their own exercise of willpower) because they had come to love the life without their sin more than the life with it. The disciplines had, at least for a time, brought a change of habit into their lives. The pattern of sin was temporarily broken. But what maintained the new pattern was love of the new life and those in it.

The Enabling Love of Change

Those with lasting health had been motivated by more than self-preservation or regret (though these were undeniably power-ful change agents too). Often their motivation was to renew and deepen a relationship with loved ones—including their Lord.

This love, more that the rigor of the disciplines themselves, was the real agent of lasting change. What the helping practitioners (and I) often considered the strength-producing power of the disciplines—which, ironically, was supposed to be generated by willpower and rigorous effort—was not really what made the disciplines effective. To assume it was would place their power in the level of human performance—a secular or even magical perspective.

Disciplined Love

What actually happened as persons began to engage in the disci-plines regularly is that the Holy Spirit ministered to them more deeply. Through the Scriptures, he taught them of God's love and grace. Through prayer, they communed with his mercy. Through fellowship and worship, they witnessed the goodness and power of his embrace. In short, the disciplines led people to a deeper, more profound, and more loving relationship with their Lord.

Displacing Love

As a result, love for the Lord more and more displaced love for their sin and the life it had created. I recognized, after many years of searching for what now seems obvious, that the *how* question (How do I find power to overcome sin?) was answered the same way as the *why* question (Why should I change?). The answer to both is "love for the Savior."

As the previous chapter explained, this is not just sentimental schmaltz. Whatever we love the most will control our lives. What ultimately changed my alcoholic young friend was not all the disciplines and accountability measures we put in place but the serious illness of his mother. When he saw what his life was doing to her and how much she needed him to be sober and helpful, his love for her began to compel his change. And when he remembered that the grace of God was greater than all his failures, misdeeds, and shame, he began to engage in Christian disciplines in a way that finally helped him.

No longer were the disciplines a measure of his willpower— of which he had none. They were an umbilical cord to the regular nourishment of the grace of God. Knowing and regularly replenishing the message of God's love and support added strength to his will that his former perception of God's judgment, frown, and distaste could never match. The disciplines stopped being sacrifices he had to offer to receive God's favor and, instead, became sustenance he longed for to refresh his joy in God's promises and power.

Bartering for Blessings

What I am suggesting is that many of us need to shift our paradigm of the usefulness of the Christian disciplines (prayer, Bible reading, and the dimensions of Christian sacraments and fellowship). For too many of us, these are a type of Christian barter: we trade our diligence and duty for God's favor and help. We muster up the effort and discipline to satisfy him and then expect him to favor us—our sweat for his sweets.

Wrong Reasons

Such use of the disciplines clearly is contrary to Scripture. The problem is not with the disciplines themselves but with our misuse of them. We are forgetting a very basic biblical premise: the right things for the wrong reasons are wrong.

In the Old Testament, the people of God sometimes offered sacrifices to God as a way of placating him while ignoring his commands and the suffering of the needy. The sacrifices offered to Jehovah were a good thing in themselves. In fact, God had commanded such sacrifices as a mark of devotion to him. But when the sacrifices were used to bribe him, God said that the smoke from the offerings was a stench in his nostrils (Isa. 1:11–14; Amos 5:12).

Senseless Bribes

If our reason for reading the Bible is so God won't get mad at us, or will be nice to us, then we are implicitly trying to buy his goodness with ours. Sometimes people even talk this way without recognizing the attitudes they are revealing: "I knew it was going to be a bad day; I didn't have a long enough quiet time."

How long would be long enough? The thought that we could use the Christian disciplines as a way of plugging faith nickels into the celestial vending machine in the sky falls apart when we remember that our best works are only polluted garments to him (Isa. 64:6). We cannot bribe God to bless us.

Our disciplines do not make us acceptable to God because they are long enough, deep enough, or frequent enough. "Enough" isn't a measure that works for an infinitely holy God.

The Bread of Change

The only way that the disciplines strengthen the Christian life is when we view them as bread, not barter. They are not trading chips to exchange for God's grace but, rather, divine manna, providing the nutrition by which our love for Christ thrives. As we meditate upon the lavishness of grace across Scripture, commune with our God in prayer, and experience many dimensions of his mercy among his people, we grow in our understanding of his love. As a consequence, our love for him grows, displacing lesser loves that attack us even as they attract us.

The Oxygen of Effort

Only as the disciplines contribute to our love for Christ—the most powerful means of healthy and lasting change—do they serve God's intended purposes. Those purposes could be compared to the oxygen a marathon runner needs to power through the final miles. Grit, determination, and willpower are also needed but will prove useless if there is no oxygen fueling the effort.

To take in the oxygen they need, runners open their mouths. They do not open wide expecting that their effort will manufacture oxygen. No effort can do that. They open their mouths to take in the oxygen already surrounding them. In the same way, we should not open the pages of Scripture, extend our hands in prayer, or reach out to other believers with the expectation that these good exercises somehow manufacture God's grace to us. His free, unbounded, unconditional grace already surrounds us and is ready to be taken in to strengthen our passion for him.

The Power of Passion

As that passion reorients the purposes, priorities, and desires of our hearts, we are empowered as well as motivated to change. When this truth became apparent to me, I realized that my long struggle to answer the *how* question was over. The question "How do I change?"—though addressed through many practical considerations and disciplines—is ultimately answered in the same way as the question "Why should I change?"

Why should we make changes in our lives that honor and please God? We change because we love him above all else. And *how* do we make changes in our lives that honor and please God? We also have the power to change when we love him above all else. When his love displaces lesser loves, they lose their power to attract us and thus lack the power to control us. When his love surpasses all others, so also does his might. The ultimate purpose of the Christian disciplines is to fill our hearts with love for Christ so that all other loves are displaced and diminished in power.

Filling with the Power of Love

When our youngest daughter was in high school, her life became incredibly busy with activities before and after classes. With my own hectic schedule, connecting with her was sometimes really hard. So my wife suggested I begin getting up early to fix Katy breakfast. Nothing extravagant—just cereal.

The cereal connection gave me frequent opportunity to consider my main responsibility as Katy's father. Of course, there were many responsibilities: give her lunch money, tell her about boys, listen to her concerns about her friends, wince at appropriate moments in her description of Mr. Tanner's math quizzes, and *please, please* pick her up on time from softball practice. All of these were important, but not the most important. I began to see my highest priority reflected in the simple process of preparing Katy's breakfast. As I was filling her cereal bowl with milk, I visualized my responsibility of filling her heart with love for Christ.

Why was that priority more important than any other? Parents know the answer. Trials and temptations were ahead. Yet, she could not be safer, stronger, or better prepared for whatever life held than when her heart was full of love for her Savior. That's the "heart chemistry" revealed in a cereal bowl—and applicable to the nurture of every child of God. A heart full of love for Christ brims with maximum motivation and power for the Christian life.

10

Just between Jesus and Me?

"So, what do you want?" The question silenced the rest of the courtroom in postapartheid South Africa, and a frail black woman rose slowly to her feet to answer. A former security officer named van der Broek had just confessed to the murder of her husband and son. The officer had come to her home under the cloak of government authority and shot her son point-blank. Then, he burned the young man's body while he and his men partied nearby.

Later the officer returned and dragged the woman's husband from her home. She did not hear from him for two years. Then the police returned one night. She was taken to a river bank where her husband, still alive but bound and beaten, was heaped on a pile of wood. He was doused with gasoline. His last words: "Father forgive them . . ." as the fire was lit.

She remembered it all, as a member of South Africa's Truth and Reconciliation Commission now addressed her in the courtroom: "So what do you want? How should justice be done to this man who so brutally destroyed your family?"

"I want three things," she replied.

I want first to be taken to the place where my husband's body was burned so that I can gather up the dust [ashes] and give his remains a decent burial.

My husband and my son were my only family. I want, secondly, for Mr. van der Broek to become my son. I would like for him to come twice a month to the ghetto and spend a day with me so that I can pour out on him whatever love I have remaining in me.

And, finally, I would like Mr. van der Broek to know that I offer him my forgiveness because Jesus died to forgive.... And so, I would kindly ask someone to come to my side and lead me across the courtroom so that I can take Mr. van der Broek in my arms, embrace him, and let him know that he is truly forgiven.

As the court assistants led the elderly woman across the room, Mr. van der Broek fainted, overwhelmed by what he had just heard.[1]

Mission of Mercy

Reading this report, many of us might first question the correctness of the woman's final requests. Should the murderer have been treated so well? Should anything else have been done for justice's sake? Is this story even true? Legitimate questions have been raised since it first circulated in Christian circles over a decade ago. And whether or not its details are accurate, does Scripture require us to respond as this forgiving woman did? Those questions must be answered in other books. My question is different but no less important: What is supposed to motivate forgiveness such as this woman offers?

---

1. Rev. Maake Masango, former moderator of the Presbyterian Church in South Africa, as related to Stanley Green (South African), president of the Mennonite Board of Missions, cited in James R. Krabill, "Fainting to the Tune of 'Amazing Grace,'" *Keep the Faith/Share the Peace* 5, no. 3 (June 1999): 1–2. On the challenge of confirming the story, see "Storytelling (Van der Broek and the Truth and Reconciliation Commission)," *Geoff's Shorts* (blog), October 28, 2011, http://geoffsshorts.blogspot.com/2011/10/storytelling-van-der-broek-and-truth.html; also Philip Yancey, reply to Richard Cronin, August 8, 2013 (3:25 a.m.), comment on "Happy Birthday, Nelson Mandela," *Philip Yancey* (blog), July 19, 2013, http://philipyancey.com/happy-birthday-nelson-mandela.

In this story, she answers, "I offer him [i.e., the murderer] my forgiveness because Jesus died to forgive." Her heart desired to share mercy that she had received through Christ's sacrifice. As simple as that may seem, it is the foundation of all Christian mission and ethics. The grace we receive changes our world so that we may be Christ's instruments of world change for those whom our lives touch.

Misunderstanding of Grace

The transforming power of grace often gets bad press. Efforts to motivate people by telling them how wonderful God's grace is *for them* often are criticized for creating egocentric Christians. The assumption is that too much focus on grace makes people selfish. They get conditioned to think only about their own personal needs (i.e., *my* forgiveness, God's mercy to *me*, and the heaven that awaits *me*).

The Math of Me

Yet, while this path of logic may appear perfectly paved for self-indulgence, the heart territory it must cross results in an entirely different destination. The manipulative math of the selfish "me" gets diluted and redirected by the chemistry of grace in the heart of a believer.

I have to concede that this concern is legitimate and its logic cannot be denied. If grace promises God's pardon for now and eternity, its recipients might well conclude, "Well, if everything is okay between Jesus and me, why bother with anyone or anything else?"

The Chemistry of Care

If we truly love Jesus, we love what and whom he loves. This may not be our natural inclination or first thought. We may have to mature in understanding as well as in love, but the end product is the same: Christ's priorities become our own.

Because I love my wife and want to please her, I listen to classical music that I don't always understand and answer questions about fabric selections that are not of great concern to me. Because she loves me, she goes on fishing trips and says, "How wonderful," no matter how small my catch. We love *what* the other loves because we love each other.

We also love each other's friends and family (though they may be outside our ordinary circles or choices). We love *whomever* the other loves because we love each other.

Jesus's loves. Whom does Jesus love? He loves the unlovely, the outcast, the needy, the lost, the poor, the orphan and widow in distress (Ps. 9:18; Isa. 16:3–5; Matt. 11:5; John 3:16; 4:35; James 1:27). He loves showing mercy and defending the powerless (Jer. 9:24; Mic. 7:18). He loves his creation, the creatures of his care, and all those made in his image (Gen. 1:25–31; 2:15; Pss. 145:8–9; 146:6–9). If we love him, we will love all of these also.

Jesus's priorities. Jesus taught us how love for him will change and channel our priorities, when he said, "Truly, I say to you, as you did it [i.e., showed care] to one of the least of these my brothers, you did it to me" (Matt. 25:40). Knowing that our care for "the least of these" is an expression of love for the Christ who loves them motivates Christian compassion.

Christ's grace toward us stimulates our love for him, which makes us want to do whatever pleases him by extending his grace toward those he loves. The consequence is counterintuitive, but very powerful.

Jesus's glory. A compromising mind may compute, "Since we are saved by grace through faith without any merit based on what we do, why should we bother to be good?" The heart throbbing with love stimulated by grace boldly answers: "So that we may show our gratitude toward the One who saved us, and bring glory to him by reflecting his grace in how we live and love others."[2]

Ethics of Grace

It is important to understand that compassionate living and loving for Christ's sake are responses to Christ's grace, not means of claiming it. A spate of recent books by well-meaning authors has rightly taken evangelical Christians to task for ignoring the ethical requirements and kingdom priorities of Scripture.

Performing Pitfalls

No one should deny that the evils of materialism, consumerism, and greed have plagued the Western church and distracted those with resources from showing needed compassion to millions suffering from poverty, war, racism, disease, malnutrition, illiteracy, addiction, slavery, trafficking, unemployment, oppression, persecution, and deprivation. Our distraction is sin and must be critiqued—and corrected.

However, to address such evil without grounding the correction in the grace that claims hearts and moves them toward biblical compassion would unintentionally create a new legalism. Christians convinced that their kingdom status is founded on their kingdom efforts will necessarily suffer from the pride or despair that afflicts all performance-based religion.

Transforming Hearts

The gospel is intended to transform our world by transforming hearts so that we will respond to the needs of those about us. But

---

2. Adapted from the Heidelberg Catechism, Q. 86.

true heart transformation is always a consequence of a spiritual change brought about by apprehension of the mercy of God toward those destined for eternal judgment apart from his grace. We must be careful not to confuse this heart response with a claim to grace. While it may well be appropriate to question whether grace has entered hearts where no compassion is evident, it is quite another thing to call others to expressions of compassion as a means of meriting grace.

Sharing His Love

If we think we can qualify to enter or secure God's kingdom by sufficient expression of Christlike care, we must recognize that however radical, selfless, or transformative our actions, they will fall short of Christ's. Until he returns, our righteousness will always be insufficient to alleviate the problems we address (Matt. 5:29; Mark 14:7). Even our best works remain filthy rags (Isa. 64:6), and when we have done all we should do, we are still unworthy of our Master's table (Luke 17:10). Heavenly hope based on our compassion undermines the gospel of hope based on Christ's compassion alone.

We must show compassion to honor our Savior, to please him, to bring the priorities of his kingdom to our world, and to make credible the grace we claim has transformed our hearts. We care for others because, in doing so, we show our love for Christ and his love for them. We do not require others to deserve our care before we express it, since we did not deserve Christ's grace when he granted it (Rom. 5:8–10; 1 John 4:10).

Priorities of Christ's Love

Always the primary aim of such expressions of our love is to communicate Christ's eternal love, even though immediate needs may require our temporal care. We provide for others' earthly needs, transforming societies at every level according to Christ's heart, and mindful that (1) heavenly religion without earthly mercy is empty (Luke 10:29–37; James 2:16), and (2) it will ultimately profit others nothing to gain even a perfect world and yet lose their souls (Matt. 16:26). So it is not a compromise to seek credibility for the gospel and good for God's world by patient, sacrificial, and creative demonstration of Christ's heart. It is compromise to prioritize others' earthly welfare over their eternal security.

Experiencing His Love

Expression of Christ's compassion for others is not merely altruistic. We also show care for others because doing so allows us to experience—not gain—more of Christ's love. The love we show is the love we know. In expressing his love selflessly and sacrificially, we sense more of the reality and depth of his love for us and, consequently, love him more (Matt. 22:36–40; 1 John 3:14–19; 4:12). Care for creation and compassion for communities bring redeeming qualities to our world, honoring Christ and demonstrating his care—to others and to our own hearts.

But none of these causes for expressing Christ's compassion *earn* it. We do not qualify for his kingdom by bringing it to life on earth. He qualifies us for his kingdom by granting us eternal life through grace from heaven. Everything we do in response is in loving thanksgiving, gratitude, and praise (Col. 3:16–17).

Advancing His Love

His grace gets us into his kingdom, maintains us in the kingdom, and secures us for the kingdom. His kingdom flourishes in and through us. We advance his kingdom's purposes and realities by our faithfulness. Of course, we have no assurance that we belong to his kingdom if nothing in us reflects his priorities (1 John 4:8, 20). But if we are kingdom citizens, it is by his grace alone (1 John 4:9–10). What we do for him is because of his grace toward us (1 John 4:11).

His love in us. That grace includes alerting us that living according to kingdom priorities is good for us (Ps. 1:1–3; Matt. 5:6–8). For example, we forgive not merely because he commands it, and not only because others may need our pardon, but also because bitterness is the acid that eats its own container.

Others have said that an unforgiving spirit is like taking poison to make someone else feel bad. The same is true of all other forms of sin. To indulge them is to destroy ourselves. Whether our lack of kingdom compassion comes in the form of unforgiveness, selfish distraction, or evil pursuit, the results are the same: barring ourselves from the experience of kingdom beauty (1 John 3:17–19).

Most of that beauty is the experience of the presence, peace, and approval of our Savior. The thought of jeopardizing any of these—once tasted—is one of sin's greatest deterrents. Thus, those who use the beauty of grace to excuse dalliance, indulgence, or ignoring of sin have not really understood grace. Nowhere does our Savior say that if we love him, we will abuse his grace, disregard his Word, ignore suffering, grieve his heart, dishonor his name, and dabble in sins that aren't too bad. Jesus said, "If you love me, you will keep my commandments" (John 14:15).

These can be difficult words to hear for many being introduced to a life motivated by grace. Our *secular* culture defines grace as license to do whatever you want. In contrast, our *church* culture often defines obedience as conformity to cultural standards that cannot be found in Scripture (e.g., retro or reflex prohibitions against certain clothing, entertainments, politics, beverages, and technologies). As a result, those who "come into grace" sometimes assume that, because grace grants freedom from such legalism, Christ has no standards to restrain us.

His love through us. Supposedly, those who "really" get grace are those who learn to cuss a little, hold their liquor, sleep around occasionally, and laugh at the dolts who don't. In reality, we could all argue that a sovereign Creator God is not likely to be terribly undone by the puffs of vocalized air that come from puny human mouths or the ounces of alcohol that go into them (Matt. 15:16–20). But God cares enormously about the relationships that are affected by all our behaviors. He thus calls those he loves to godliness in speech, moderation in all consumptions, purity in relationships, and respect for all who are made in his image (Eph. 5:18; 2 Tim. 2:16; Heb. 13:4).

And lest we be culturally limited in our corrections to legalism, we should also remember that grace does not excuse materialism, favoritism, cynicism, racism, gossip, disrespect of leaders, disregard for creation, ignoring the destitute, irreverence, immodesty, or indolence (Acts 17:24; Rom. 13:1–5; 2 Cor. 12:20; Eph. 2:14–22; 2 Thess. 3:10; 1 Tim. 2:9; Heb. 13:5; James 2:1–17; 1 John 4:20). That list should break us all, making us profoundly aware of our need for the grace of our Savior and deeply grateful for its free and infinite supply.

Christ's grace alone is our hope, but it is meant for more than us alone. As we perceive how wonderful is the mercy of the Savior who rescues us from all our sin, we delight to delight him. Nothing does this more than living so that others may know and experience his love through us.

Grace is a calling to Christlikeness as we reflect the One we love because he first loved us (Titus 2:11–14). In so living, we not only bless his name; we also bless what and whom he loves: his creation and his creatures. Nothing so floods our hearts with the experience of God's grace as making sure it overflows from our hearts.

Part 2

FINDING HEART CHEMISTRY IN THE BIBLE

11

Grace Everywhere

In his high school years, my oldest son, Colin, became a rock hound, learning how to collect and identify semiprecious stones and minerals. One day he took me to a creek bed renowned for its geodes—rocks with beautiful crystal formations hidden inside their plain exteriors.

At first, all I could see were thousands of nondescript brown rocks. Then Colin taught me what distinguished the geodes—their shape, contour, and color. I spotted a few. But then, as I got familiar with their patterns, I began to see more geodes. The more my identification skills improved, the more geodes I found. Ultimately, I began to see that the geodes were everywhere around me. They had been there all along; I just hadn't been prepared to see them.

Finding Grace in Scripture

So far in this book, we have considered how important the grace of God is to motivate and enable Christian obedience. But where do we find all this grace? In much of the Bible the word *grace* isn't used, and Jesus doesn't always talk about it. Some people even teach that

the Old Testament's revelation of God is different from the New
Testament's and that his grace doesn't emerge until Jesus dies.

In order to stir the heart chemistry of Christian obedience from
all of Scripture, we must learn to see that Christ's grace does not
wait until the last chapters of Matthew to appear. Like the geodes
that my son helped me to find, grace is everywhere in the Bible. We
just have to learn to see it.

Different Details

We won't see grace everywhere in the pages of Scripture if we expect it to look exactly the same in every place. As geodes take time
to develop and come in different varieties and sizes, grace develops
and unfolds in various ways. It has consistent patterns, but no two
expressions of grace are exactly the same.

Same Theme

The message of grace becomes more obvious and brilliant as
Christ's ministry approaches, begins, and expands. The theme of
God's willingness to rescue people who cannot rescue themselves
from spiritual ruin unfolds from Scripture's earliest pages. Jesus's
ministry and message should not have been a surprise. He himself
made this clear when he spoke to the religious leaders of his day,
saying, "You search the Scriptures because you think that in them
you have eternal life; and it is they that bear witness about me"
(John 5:39; see also 1:45).

After his resurrection, Jesus spoke similarly to his disciples on
the road to Emmaus. Luke records Jesus's conversation this way:
"And beginning with Moses and all the Prophets, he interpreted to
them in all the Scriptures the things concerning himself" (Luke
24:27; see also v. 44). Jesus says repeatedly that all the Scriptures
bear witness of him. But of course, a key question remains: How

do they do this? Jesus cannot be contending that all portions of Scripture directly mention him. Most verses and most accounts in the Bible make no explicit reference to Jesus.

The Big Picture

We will understand what Jesus meant about all Scripture bearing witness to him as we remember the big picture of the Bible. An old cliché says, "History is 'his story.'" But how is this story of Jesus unfolding across the past and future millennia as described in the Bible?

A standard way of thinking about the big picture of God's dealing with humanity begins with a good creation, which is then spoiled by Adam's fall, then is redeemed by Christ's provision, and finally is perfected in the consummation of Christ's rule over all things. God's world and people were made good, went bad, are being redeemed, and will be made perfect. This creation-fall-redemption-consummation perspective helps us map all the events of Scripture. All have a place in this great unfolding plan of "his story" because he is the central figure to whom they point. He made everything good (John 1:3; Col. 1:16), was promised to us when everything went bad (Gen. 3:15; Acts 13:32–33; Rom. 16:20), is the culmination of God's redemption (or rescue) plan (Acts 2:23; 26:22–23; 1 Pet. 1:20), and makes everything he has redeemed perfect with his ultimate reign (1 Cor. 15:24–28; Rev. 21:1–8).

The Great Rescue

In addition to seeing the overall plan of "his story," it is important to remember that the "rescue" component of biblical history begins unfolding long before the crucifixion narrative in the Gospels. The Bible reveals the dawning light of Christ's gracious rescue plan near its very beginning.

Setting the Stage

Immediately after Adam and Eve sinned, God said to the one who tempted them,

> I will put enmity between you and the woman,
>   and between your offspring and her offspring;
> he shall bruise your head,
>   and you shall bruise his heel. (Gen. 3:15)

Bible scholars refer to this verse as the "first gospel." It is God's first promise to redeem his world and people—broken by Adam's sin—by divine provision. God promised to send One who would come through a human source to defeat Satan even while experiencing an awful attack from him. Satan would bruise the heel of the coming Savior, causing his suffering; but the Savior would bruise the head of Satan, crushing his influence.

This early verse in Genesis sets the stage for all that follows in the Bible. The rest of human history will be played out on this stage. Thus, every portion of Scripture thereafter has a redemptive context. Our goal as faithful Bible readers is not to try to make Jesus magically appear in every text, but to see where every text fits in this redemptive epic. Jesus is the culmination and climax of the whole story. So the stage is set for him; all that transpires on the stage relates to him; and we do not *fully* understand anything on the stage until we have identified its relation to him.

Seeing His Grace

Placing every text in its redemptive context does not mean we have to force every verse somehow to mention Jesus. We shouldn't need decoder rings or a computer program to figure out God's core message. God's purpose is very plain. Every text relates some aspect of God's redeeming grace that finds its fullest expression in Christ.

Grace emerges on the page whenever God provides for people who cannot provide for themselves. Most often these reflections of God's provision do not reveal the full story of Christ's work of salvation, but signal aspects of his mercy and mission that other Scripture more fully reveals.

When God provides food for the hungry, strength for the weary, family for the fatherless, faithfulness to the faithless, forgiveness for the undeserving, and a thousand other glimpses of his grace, he is revealing dimensions of his character and care that become fully embodied in the provision of his Son. Ultimately, we understand who Christ is and what he does by how he fleshes out the message of God's redemption that unfolds throughout the Bible.

This unfolding gospel perspective may be communicated in a variety of ways in the Bible. Many texts specifically describe, prophesy, or typify (set a pattern for) the ministry of Jesus. Straightforward identification of obvious gospel truths is sufficient for understanding these texts. There are many more texts, however, that prepare for or reflect upon Christ's ministry by disclosing aspects of the grace of God that find their completed expression in Jesus.

A Variety of Windows

These "gospel windows" reveal God's gracious nature and provision through a variety of logical and literary means. For example:

Contexts. Before we try to figure out what a biblical text is about, we should identify where it fits in biblical history. Are we early or late in the story of God's plan of redemption? Are we in a place where people are rebelling, or where God is rescuing, or where some other aspect of God's grace is shown to be needed or supplied? Getting the context right helps us see what aspect of grace God's people needed then, and why we need it in similar contexts.

If we miss the context, we might end up telling people, "You should try to be as strong and smart as Samson," when the real message in the context of the book of Judges is that people who depend on their own strength and cleverness get in a lot of trouble, and only God can get them out.

Themes. When we see a recurring theme, image, or pattern of God's grace, we see how God is weaving together the story of his love so that we will recognize its implications and respond appropriately. A theme or image typical of God's redemptive work can carry right through the Old and New Testaments. When God rescued his people from slavery by the blood of a Passover lamb in the book of Exodus, he was teaching them that sacrifice would be needed for their redemption. So the New Testament writers frequently use the Passover lamb to explain Christ's person and work. Themes and images from the garden of Eden, the temple of the Old Testament, the kingship of David, and many other Old Testament accounts echo in the New Testament to help us understand why we need Jesus and what he needed to do. He will restore the peace of the garden that our sin destroyed; he provides the sacrifice our sin deserves so that we may be the temple he desires; and he is the better Davidic King who shepherds our lives with righteousness and compassion.

Truths. Sometimes accounts in the Old Testament, as well as the New, identify doctrinal truths that become foundational to our gospel understanding. For example, the apostle Paul explained salvation by faith with the reminder that Abraham believed God and it was credited to him for righteousness (Gen. 15:6; cf. Rom. 4:3, 22). Many times truths about the nature of God's grace are planted in an Old Testament account and flourish in New Testament explanations.

Actions. A redemptive reading of a passage may simply show how God's divine care for his people demonstrates characteristics of grace. When God gives victory to a weakling, or treasures a treacherous nation, or feeds a fleeing prophet, or comforts a cowardly king, or warns the undeserving, or receives anyone's repentance—in all these cases and all the other accounts where God provides the help that humanity needs but cannot supply or deserve, we learn about his redemptive nature. The stories are not random. They display grace so we will learn to recognize it, depend upon it, and trust the One who offers it.

Promises. Through covenants, predictions, and prophesies God communicates care for his people that transcends our time and knowledge. Through covenants he commits himself to care for people who will not and cannot keep their commitments. Through predictions he demonstrates knowledge and power that supersede human wisdom and weakness. Through prophesies he proves that he is faithful beyond our crises, failures, and false messiahs. Through all these aspects of his future faithfulness he makes and fulfills promises that enable us to trust him and turn to him beyond the limitations of our wisdom, vision, and world. That's grace too.

Allegorical Views

Identifying the unfolding grace of Scripture in these faithful ways differs from some past approaches that tried to mash Jesus onto every page of the Old Testament. Some interpreters understood Christ's statements about all the Scriptures speaking of him to justify concocting fantastic and fanciful references to Jesus from Old Testament passages.

These allegorical interpretations relied a great deal on human imagination to make claims that, for example, the wood of Noah's ark symbolizes the wood of the cross, or the water of the parted Red

Sea prefigures the water that would come from Christ's side on the cross. The good intention was to show that God had revealed Christ's coming many centuries before, but the explanations often rested more on human creativity than on any provable divine intention.

Someone could just as easily say that the wood of Noah's ark represents the wood of the manger, the carpenter's shop, the ark of the covenant, the paneling of the temple of Israel, or the boat from which Christ stilled the storm. The water of the parted sea could be thought to represent the sea calmed by the Savior, the water turned into wine at his mother's request, the baptism he received, or the baptisms his disciples administered.

The trouble with all such allegorical interpretations is their lack of support in biblical revelation. Maybe they make sense—maybe not. But either way, no scriptural authority can be logically established for their claims against other possible interpretations.

Biblical Guidance

If the New Testament does not indicate that a specific object or account is about Jesus, it is best not to force an interpretation on other grounds. At the same time, we should be very willing to learn principles of redemptive interpretation that the New Testament writers employed and exemplified.

In the next chapter we will explore these principles so that we can rightly excavate grace from any portion of Scripture in order to stir the heart chemistry from which Christian faithfulness arises. The goal is not simply to improve our interpretive skills—or to show that we are now just a little smarter—but to learn to see the grace that really helps people change. When we see how long and wide and high and deep is the love of God in his Word, then we will love and trust and turn to him more—and will help others to do the same (Eph. 3:18).

12

Grace Excavated

My pastoral ministry began with a great privilege. I was asked to lead a historic church. Though I delighted in the honor, I soon discovered that I was not prepared for the problems or the pain of my privileged position.

The church was in a mining and farming community being ravaged by economic woes. The mines were closing and the farms were dying. Sin was not. As jobs and incomes went down, the repercussions of family stress skyrocketed: drug use, alcohol dependency, promiscuity, abuse, divorce, and depression—everywhere depression shrouded our lives.

I thought I knew what to do. I had been taught that God's Word corrects those who struggle with sinful dependencies, activities, and depression. So I would point in my Bible to where all such ungodliness was condemned, and I would preach, "Stop it!"

With clear explanations of the biblical text, I would thunder, "You know that the Bible condemns what you are doing. So, just stop it." I said "Stop it" so often that I could not stand me anymore. One day I told my wife, "I can't do this anymore. I didn't go to seminary to learn to hurt people, but I stand in the pulpit every Sunday and I do hurt people."

I began to take steps to leave the ministry. Then the Lord graciously intervened. He brought a book into my life—by means I cannot now recall—that discussed a centuries-old controversy.[1]

The Heroes of the Bible

The controversy was about how we should teach the heroes of the Bible. Do we basically say, "They were good, and you should be good too?" Or do we honestly acknowledge the feet of clay of virtually every human figure?

Is it honest to declare David's victory over Goliath and never mention David's sin with Bathsheba, or the murder of her husband, or the rebellion of David's children, or the preening pride that plagued the end of his life? If we simply encourage people to be like David when he was good, are we teaching all the Bible intends for us to know about him?

One True Hero

The point of the book examining this controversy was that there is only one true hero in the Bible. His name is Jesus. Everyone else is remarkably human—flawed, sinful, and (even when good) desperately needing God's help to express the faithfulness that distinguished their lives.

To proclaim the heroes apart from the grace of God that enabled their heroism, or pardoned behavior less noble, warps the biblical message. God did not wait until the New Testament to display his grace. Throughout the Scriptures he demonstrates his saving nature by using people as flawed as David, Abraham, the

1. Sidney Greidanus, *Sola Scriptura: Problems and Principles in Preaching Historical Texts* (Toronto: Wedge, 1970).

apostles, and many others to bring salvation to equally messed-up people.

Perhaps that message is obvious to some. For years, it was not to me. I read the Bible with the primary goals of determining the good behavior or correct doctrine it taught. Identifying the grace that covered inadequate performance or inferior competence was not on my radar. Only when grace began to beacon did I stop reading past the realities of human weakness. And only then did a radical revision of my preaching occur.

Use for the Useless

I realized that instead of constantly repeating "Stop it" to God's people, I had another message—summoned from the same Bible but far more helpful. I could say with biblical integrity, "If God can use people as messed up as David (and so many other biblical characters), he can still use people as messed up as you—and me."

I needed that message of grace as much as anyone hearing my preaching. I wasn't out of my twenties but already believed that I was a failure. Though I had been given a great privilege of leading a historic church at an early age, the challenges had broken me. No one needed new hope more than I. When I began to see the grace that filled the Bible, I began to believe that God could still have a purpose for me.

Fuel for Life

As I claimed that grace, God's people began to cling to the hope I began to share from the pulpit. The Holy Spirit blessed words more true to his purposes. Surprising joy began to replace pervasive depression. And with that joy came new zeal for God's Word and ways.

I began to realize that giving people hope from the Bible was as important as giving instruction. I also began to understand that *all* Scripture is designed to give us this hope by consistently revealing the grace that culminates in the person and work of Christ (Rom. 15:4). This grace, as the earlier portions of this book have discussed, is motivation and power for the Christian life. Revealing grace in all of Scripture does not compromise our commitments to Christian duty and doctrine, but fuels them.

Drilling for Grace Honestly

Of course, the key question now is how we drill for this fuel without contaminating the message each passage of the Bible is intended to teach. Whether you serve others as a pastor, Sunday school teacher, counselor, parent, or friend, you should want to teach what the Bible says without imposing meanings the Holy Spirit did not inspire. (The rest of this chapter provides the thought foundation for excavating grace from every kind of biblical text. If it gets a little heavy for you, feel free to go to the next chapter—the summary version is there!)

Recognize What's Different

How do we find grace without forcing it upon the text? First, we should remember (as discussed in the previous chapter) that not all texts reveal grace in the same way. Sometimes the Bible reveals its truths in prophecies, but it also instructs us through poetry, proverbs, histories, and letters. We will need a variety of approaches to help us to see the unfolding message of grace among the various types of Scripture. But even these different approaches share common ground.

Ask What's Wrong

Already we have seen that all Scripture is written in the context of God's plan to redeem his people from their fallen world. That means we can start thinking redemptively about any text in the Bible by asking, "What went wrong here?" or "What is the human struggle that the Holy Spirit is addressing?"

Even if the text only describes good things for us to know or do (such as praising God's splendor and steadfast love), we should ask, "Why do we need this instruction—what's the problem with us that necessitated God reminding us of something so basic?" Focusing on an aspect of our fallen condition will point us toward the grace God must provide to rescue, restore, or redeem us. In essence, we identify the hole we are in (what I call elsewhere the Fallen Condition Focus) so that we will appreciate the ladder God is providing to get us out.[2]

Ladders for Our Understanding

In order for us to take hold of the ladder of God's grace, we have to know that it gets lowered to us in different ways. Various aspects of God's Word *predict, prepare for, result from,* or *reflect* the person and/or work of Christ.

These four categories of gospel explanation are not meant to be exhaustive. There are other good ways to see grace. And it's best not to think that we have to keep these categories rigidly separate. These are just tools to help us explain how all Scripture points to Christ's nature and/or work.

The Prediction Ladder

Some passages—such as the prophecies and the messianic psalms—clearly *predict* who Christ is and what he will do. Isaiah wrote of the Messiah:

> His name shall be called
> Wonderful Counselor, Mighty God,

---

2. See Bryan Chapell, *Christ-Centered Preaching: Redeeming the Expository Sermon*, 2nd ed. (Grand Rapids, MI: Baker, 2005), 48–54.

> Everlasting Father, Prince of Peace.
> Of the increase of his government and of peace
>   there will be no end. (Isa. 9:6–7)

Zechariah said that our King would one day come "humble and mounted on a donkey" (Zech. 9:9).

These are clear predictions of Jesus's person and work, and there are many more—relating to both his first and second comings. If we are reading or teaching from these texts, we should understand that our rescue is through God's provision and not our own. This is the nature of the grace that the prophets reveal in many dimensions.

The Preparation Ladder

Other passages *prepare* God's people to understand the grace that God must ultimately provide for them through Christ. For example, David was chosen by God to represent his rule for the covenant people. So when God uses King David to show mercy to Saul's lame grandson (a royal descendant who would be David's blood rival for Israel's throne), we understand something about the gracious character of God that will be revealed in Christ.

The Israelite king who serves and represents God shows mercy toward enemies and helps the helpless. We don't have to find a "secret code" for Jesus in this account to begin to understand the gracious character of David's future King, and our Lord.

Bridges of understanding. Not only do many Old Testament passages prepare God's people to understand the grace of *his provision*; they also prepare his people to understand *their need*. For example, Paul writes in Galatians 3:24 that the law was our schoolmaster or guardian helping to lead us to Christ.

The high and holy standards of God's law break our hope that human performance will make us acceptable to a holy God. While they teach us appropriate moral conduct, they simultaneously prepare us to seek his mercy. This grace pattern is knit into not only Moses's Ten Commandments but also Jesus's Sermon on the Mount and all the standards of holiness the prophets and apostles teach.

The sacrifice system of the Old Testament further prepares us to understand that without the shedding of blood there is no atonement for sin (Heb. 9:22). And because Abraham's faith was counted to him as righteousness, we are prepared to see that our standing before God depends upon our faith in the provision of another (Rom. 4:23–24). These are only a few of the many ways the Bible prepares our hearts for grace by bridging our understanding of God's ancient provision to his present grace.

Dead-end signs. In addition to these Old Testament *bridges* to New Testament truths of grace, God also prepares us for Christ's ministry by showing us *dead ends* to avoid. As people in Scripture take wrong turns time and again through their dependence on false prophets, wayward priests, and faulty kings, we learn of our need for a better Prophet, Priest, and King. The Old Testament histories of vain judges, law-breaking people, and flawed leaders are not teaching of heroism that merits grace, but of grace that must come through a superior Judge, a perfect law keeper, and the only unflawed hero. The messed-up people in the Bible are not there by mistake. Their stories are gracious road signs warning us that self-reliance is a dead end.

Grace does not spring up in the New Testament like a surprise jack-in-the-box. God's people have been prepared for millennia to understand and receive the grace of Christ. We will best comprehend and teach these preparatory passages when we not only identify the good behaviors they teach but also identify the God who enabled the heroes we admire, and prepared a Redeemer for those less admirable. Learning to identify both the bridges and the dead ends of Scripture's road map is important preparation for the gracious journey God intends for his people.

The Result Ladder

God's redemptive message also appears in texts that are a *result* of Christ's work in our behalf. We are justified, sanctified, adopted, and glorified as a result of Christ's atoning work and spiritual indwelling. Our prayers are heard as a result of his priestly intercession for us. Our wills are transformed as a result of our union with him. We worship as a result of God's gracious provision for every aspect of our salvation.

Provision before performance. Ultimately, reading Scripture with an eye to understanding how our status and actions result from grace does two things: (1) it reminds us that apart from Christ we can do nothing; and (2) it keeps straight the order of our identity and God's imperatives (see more extensive discussion of these in chaps. 3–4).

If the only message we take from a particular passage is that Christians should do better and know more, then we have missed the point being made by the broader context of the passage—indeed by the totality of Scripture. As I mentioned before, every other faith teaches that people must make their way to God by some discipline of body or mind, but Christianity alone teaches that such a journey is impossible.

From its earliest pages to its final verse, the Bible makes clear that our fallen condition prevents us all from ever being able to make our way to God by depending on our performance or competence. Instead, the unique claim of the Christian faith is that God reaches down to enable us to come to him by the provision of his Son. Through faith in him alone, God unites us to himself.

Results from gratitude. Messages without grace turn us from hope in God's provision to reliance on whatever human resources we can muster. Messages seasoned with grace produce grateful hearts filled with the desire to please God. And hearts filled with this priority are motivated to employ the spiritual resources our risen Lord provides through his indwelling Spirit and imparted gifts (Eph. 4:8–12; Col. 3:15–16).

When the apostles wrote to the first churches, their letters typically began with the doctrinal explanation of the grace God provided through the work of Christ. The second part of their letters then spoke of the spiritual and moral obligations that resulted from God's provision. The pattern reminds us not only that obedience is impossible apart from the grace of God, but also that true obedience is built upon God's gracious provision (Eph. 2:8–10).

Response to grace. By God's grace alone, we are made members of his eternal family. We cannot earn a right to heaven but, rather, are granted its privileges. By grace we have the identity of forgiven children of heaven's King. Lives devoted to honoring God and obeying his commands build on the identity he gives, not the status our works merit. So, when we teach obedience to the imperatives of Scripture, we need to make sure that we present it as our response to God's grace, not a means to claim it.

Inside-out identity. We must never teach or imply (by citing Scripture's imperatives apart from the grace that is their foundation and fuel) that our identity before God is based on our behavior. We "behave" because we *are* his dearly loved children, not to *become* his children (Eph. 5:1).

God transforms us from the inside out graciously giving us hearts that are willing and able to live for him. He does not love us because of what we do. We do what he loves because we love the

One who loves us despite our doing. Because he will never forsake us, even when we fail him, we never *want* to fail him (Rom. 5:10; Heb. 13:5).

The Reflection Ladder

Because grace is so key to understanding Scripture's message culminating in Christ, aspects of his gospel are *reflected* throughout the Bible.

Two key questions. When a text does not plainly predict, prepare for, or result from Christ's person or work, then redemptive truths reflected in the text can always be discerned by asking two questions:

1. What does this text reflect about the nature of God who provides redemption?
2. What does this text reflect about the nature of humanity that requires redemption?

In essence, we ask, (1) What does this text tell me about *God*? and (2) What does this text tell me about *me*? These are fair questions to ask of any text. They do not require great leaps of imagination or improper imposing of New Testament perspectives on Old Testament texts. Yet, these simple questions are lenses that will enable us to see gospel truths beaconing in any passage.

With these questions we are *not* asking, "What symbol of Jesus is here?" or "What event in Christ's life is prefigured here?" or even "What concept from the New Testament must I import into this Old Testament text to interpret it correctly?" By simply asking, "What does this text teach about *God* and *me*?" we will see something distinctive about his nature and ours—something that separates us unless he unites us to himself—something we require that he alone can provide. In the command "You shall not steal [anything great or small—ever]" (Ex. 20:15), I ultimately see reflected that God is holy and that I am a thief requiring his pardon and provision. In a psalm that urges consistent praise of God, I learn that he is worthy of praise, and that I struggle to offer it apart from his intervention in my heart.

The provision may be specifically named in the text, or we may need to discern it by identifying the human need that requires God's aid. The result will be the same: inevitably these lenses will help us see that God alone supplies the grace we need but cannot provide for ourselves. Even if there is no direct mention of Jesus— and most of the time there will not be—the text will lead us forward in our understanding of the grace that our Redeemer must supply (Acts 20:24; 1 Cor. 2:2; Gal. 3:24).

Gospel glasses. Together these lenses (the two key questions) function as gospel glasses to help us see basic truths of unfolding grace (e.g., God is holy and we are not, God is sovereign and we are vulnerable, God is merciful and we require his mercy). Such reading glasses always make us aware of our need of God's grace to compensate for our sin and inability.

Using these glasses throughout the Old and New Testaments will enable us to see the gracious nature of God, who provides redemption as he gives strength to the weak, rest to the weary, deliverance to the disobedient, faithfulness to the unfaithful, food to the hungry, salvation to sinners, and more (see chap. 11). As we see that God provides what we humans cannot provide for ourselves, grace glistens throughout the biblical record.

We also learn about humanity's need for redemption when our lenses reveal that biblical heroes fail, patriarchs lie, kings fall, prophets cower, disciples doubt, and covenant people become idolaters. Our gospel glasses prevent us from portraying biblical characters *only* as moral heroes to emulate. Rather, we will see them as the Holy Spirit intended—flawed men and women who needed the grace of God as much as we do.

Every text, seen in its redemptive context, reflects an aspect of humanity's fallen condition that requires the grace of God. Focus upon this fallen condition will inevitably crush us until we consider the accompanying revelations of divine grace that culminate in the provision of the Savior. Then, we soar into the joy that is our strength (Neh. 8:10).

Living in Grace

Since God's love for us is the soil in which love for God grows, identifying his grace in all Scripture is not simply a nice or novel approach. Regular exposure to grace ignites love for God, which is his greatest command and our greatest compulsion (Matt. 22:37–38; 2 Cor. 5:14).

We identify the grace pervading Scripture in order to fan into flame our zeal for the Savior. Our goal is not merely good interpretation but stimulation of a profound love for God that bears holy fruit. As honoring the One we love above all becomes our greatest delight, it also becomes our greatest motivation and the power for a life that glorifies him (Neh. 8:10; 1 Cor. 10:31).

Part 3

ANSWERING HEART CHEMISTRY'S KEY QUESTIONS

13

How to Find Grace in Every Passage

I recognize that the previous chapter (the longest in this book) has dealt with the question of how to excavate grace from the entire Bible. But those explanations were necessarily long and a little complex so that I could do justice to the depth and variety of biblical texts. Sometimes you will need the more refined tools of that chapter, but here's a simple method that will quickly get you to the same place most of the time. I am going to repeat some things but in a way that gives you ready access to the grace glowing in every text.

Put on Your Gospel Glasses

When you read a passage of Scripture, be sure to put on your gospel glasses. Remember, that means simply looking at the text through lenses formed by two questions: (1) What does this text tell me about the nature of God who provides redemption; and (2) What does this text tell me about the nature of humanity that requires redemption. Or more simply, ask, "What does this text tell me about God?" and "What does this text tell me about me?" That's not so hard.

But it's also important, when you ask these questions, to have an idea what answers to expect. As the saying goes, "If you go looking for apples, you are not going to find oranges." So if we are looking for grace, what are we likely to see?

Look for the Gap

If you expect to find some deep theological treatise in the text, you may well give up on your new glasses. Instead, look for the "gap"— some distance or disparity between God's nature and ours. That's a lot easier to spot. If you look for aspects of God's nature, you will quickly notice that the passage somehow shows him as holy, righteous, and good. At the same time, you'll see that we are not—at least, not until God has worked in our hearts.

But this gap between God's holiness and our unholiness is not the only thing our gospel glasses will reveal. They will also reveal that God is doing something about the gap. In some way in the passage, God is closing the gap. He is the hero, providing the resources, resolve, revelation, or rescue that is needed, and thereby revealing his grace. He is providing what humanity needs but cannot provide for itself. That's grace!

Look for the Hero

Most of the time, we can find the grace in the text by asking, "How is God coming to the rescue?" We usually know we have spotted grace in the text if we can explain how God is the ultimate hero. Even if there are human heroes, we should make clear that their heroism results from God's grace. Their resources, wisdom, courage, opportunity, or resolve come from God. We need never deny that the human heroes are heroic, but we must never forget that they are human. Apart from God's grace, they could do nothing (John 15:5).

Spotting grace in this way first means that we will not always see grace as the full revelation of Jesus's life, death, and resurrection. The Bible unfolds the message of grace across the centuries. The message is not full-blown in the Old Testament. It builds to its culmination in Christ. We see more and more of God's grace as the Bible progresses, so that when Jesus appears, we understand his gracious nature and work.

Look for the Glimmers

This means that grace may just glimmer in many Old Testament passages before it blazes in the New Testament. Every time God gives strength to the weak, food to the hungry, rest to the weary, freedom to slaves, return to exiles, faithfulness to the unfaithful, his Word to the forgetful, his love to the unlovely, his forgiveness to the sinful, and all the other blessings that humanity cannot provide for itself, we are learning about the grace that reaches its full glory in Jesus.

Seeing grace unfolding this way (from glimmers to glory) in all of Scripture also keeps us from trying to make grace magically appear with allegorical references to Christ or the cross. Allegorical interpretation depends more on our imagination than on good Scripture principles. It tries to make the wood of Noah's ark represent the cross of Christ, and the Red Sea waters transform into the wine of the Lord's Supper. Good intentions do not excuse bad interpretations. There is no scriptural logic that proves these specific conclusions were ever intended (or are the only possibilities), but there is great opportunity in these accounts to point out how God's rescue of Noah and the Israelites definitely represents his gracious nature. If we will use our gospel glasses to see and share the simple grace that is present, we will interpret the Bible as God intended.

Look at the Context

But what if there is no grace mentioned in the passage? What if the text is simply a command or a long list of things to do? Think of passages like Psalm 150 (which tells us all the ways we should praise God), or the Ten Commandments (which tell us all kinds of things *not* to do), or Romans 12:9–21 (which tells us all kinds of things to do)?

Here are two pointers: (1) look for grace in the spiritual background; and (2) look for grace in the historical or literary context.

The Spiritual Background

We discover the spiritual background by asking a *why* question of the text. So, if there are a lot of commands, such as "Let everything that has breath praise the Lord!" (Ps. 150:6), then ask, "*Why* does God give this command?" The answer cannot simply be that we need this instruction as information. God intends for us to follow his command. And the fact that he must give it, explain it, and repeatedly remind us of it indicates that our worship needs help. He is infinitely worthy of worship, and we hardly ever offer it as we should. There's a gap there—one that God graciously closes by instructing us how we can and should worship him. He doesn't leave us wondering or wandering. He leads us to himself and helps us with the worship that glorifies him and blesses us. That, again, is grace.

The Historical Context

Grace may also be evident in the historical context of the commands. In a text like Exodus 20:1–17 (the Ten Commandments), God reminds his people that their obedience is a result of his rescue. Before he gives a single command, he reminds them, "I am the Lord your God, who brought you out of the land of Egypt, out of the house of slavery" (Ex. 20:2). What's so gracious about that statement? The answer becomes apparent when you think about the order of God's words and work. He never said, "You obey me, and *then* I will release you from slavery." He never made his people's actions the prerequisite for his care. He acted in their behalf before they acted in obedience.

God's words reflect the history of his work in this situation. His care came before his commands—and continued beyond his people's faithfulness. The historical context of the commands reveals God's gracious nature and needs to be explained along with the commands, lest people think that their obedience causes God to be gracious. That's true of this passage and the many other historical passages of the Bible that place commands in the context of God's redeeming work.

The Literary Context

Grace may also be evident in the literary context of a passage. For example, Romans 12:9–21 has many commands for New Testament believers. But this letter of the apostle Paul does not contain a lot of historical information about the church in Rome. What the letter does contain is an extensive explanation of what God has done to redeem his people through the work of Jesus Christ. The commands follow the chapters that explain God's redeeming grace. The letter is designed to make our obedience a loving response to God's unmerited favor.

The literary structure of Paul's letter to the Romans (and virtually all the other epistles of the New Testament) teaches the same message as the Ten Commandments: God's care precedes his commands. Our obedience is how we respond to his grace, not how we earn it. The literary context reveals God's grace and how God's people respond to it. Two takeaways for us: (1) grace does not eliminate God's commands; and (2) God's commands should not be taught without their gracious context.

What Is Not Enough

In order to interpret biblical instructions properly, we have to find the grace that is their context. If we will put on our gospel glasses, the grace will become apparent. It's not enough simply to say *what* happened or *what* God required. We need to discover the grace that is present so we can show *why* the Holy Spirit provided the text and *how* we are to respond. Somehow God intends to inspire, encourage, humble, or instruct us with his grace so that we will love and follow him. Grace stimulates our love and loyalty. Understanding those purposes leads us to our next few questions about how grace affects our application of biblical texts.

14

How to Avoid Legalism

If grace does not erase God's commands, how does it affect the way we teach them? Can we really insist on obedience to God's laws without becoming legalistic and implying that his affection depends on our performance? These questions really boil down to our understanding of the purpose of God's commands. Are they given so that we might experience his love freely offered to us, or so that we might *earn* his love? Since our best works are like a "polluted garment" to him (Isa. 64:6), we know that earning divine affection is always beyond us. This must mean that God has given his law so that we will experience, not earn, the good he intends for our lives. That goal reminds us to keep his grace in the foundation of all biblical instruction.

Beware of the Deadly "Be"

Already we have discussed why Christian explanations of the Bible should not settle for simple instruction to be like some biblical hero (see chap. 12). The Bible actually seems intent on tarnishing the reputations of almost all its heroes. That's because we are supposed to recognize there is only one true hero. His name is Jesus. Recognizing his unique nature should help us avoid any message that passes for biblical instruction but is actually deadly to the Christian spirit. I call this sort of message a Deadly "Be."

"Be Like"

Messages whose entire instruction is some version of "be like" this or that noble biblical character fail because the full story of any character typically reveals awful flaws. The patriarchs lied and connived, the judges were cruel and cowardly, the kings coveted and caved to sinful pressures, the prophets ranted and ran, and the apostles betrayed and ran too. Of course, their failures are not the full story, but neither is their righteousness. They all required big doses of grace to fulfill God's purposes for their lives.

Teaching the Whole Truth

We are supposed to learn from and follow the exemplary features of biblical heroes' lives, but not to ignore their humanity. If we tell only the good stuff and say to people, "You should be like that," then we short the biblical message and mislead our listeners. The good stuff happened because God blessed beyond human effort and achievement. While he teaches us good behavior and paths of blessing through the lives of biblical characters, he also teaches us that human creatures need divine help to live that way. That's where grace comes in.

Teaching people merely to be like some good feature of a biblical character's life is not wrong *in* itself, but it is wrong *by* itself. Such instruction implies that God's approval and our righteousness are simply matters of our having sufficient wisdom and willpower. That's definitely not the message of the Bible with its consistent refrain of humanity's fallen nature.

Avoiding Pride and Despair

Teaching people to be like a noble person in the Bible without dependence upon the grace that person needed to be noble only creates pride (in those who think they can) and despair (in those who know they can't). If you want to test that conclusion, ask people what they think of their responsibility to "be like Jesus." Beware of those who think they can. Show grace to those who know they cannot. God gives us the example of his Son so that we will model our ways after his heart, but never by forgetting how much we need his grace to do so.

"Be Good"

Very similar to "be like" messages are "be good" messages. Now, how could there possibly be anything wrong with telling people to be good? We certainly don't want to tell them to be bad! Actually there is nothing wrong with a "be good" message—unless that's all you say.

Avoiding Spiritual Poison

Clearly the Bible has many "be good" messages in its pages. The commands, the examples, and the concerns for our care of others consistently direct us toward holy living. God even says, "Be holy, for I am holy" (Lev. 11:44). But there's the problem. Holiness is the result of absolute purity. A holy person has absolutely no faults or flaws—ever. How could we possibly be holy apart from God's provision? He also tells us, "None is righteous, no, not one" (Rom. 3:10). So, if he doesn't enable our holiness, we will never accumulate enough good works to be good enough for a holy God.

Many a well-meaning Sunday school teacher has tried to encourage good behavior this way: "Oh, Jessica, if you are just a good little girl, Jesus will love you." The words are spoken gently and sweetly but are spiritual poison (see also chap. 4). Jesus loves us not because we are good but because he is. To teach any child that God's love depends on our goodness is spiritually damaging.

Embracing the Christian Distinction

Christianity is distinct. Unlike all other religions of the world, it does not teach that any level of human goodness, effort, or mental transcendence will enable us to reach heaven. As high as the heavens are above the earth, so beyond us are God's holy standards (1 Sam. 2:2; Isa. 6:1–3). In order for us to unite with him, he must reach down to us. He did so through the person and work of Jesus. To teach that our goodness will get us to God apart from his grace is not simply sub-Christian (saying less than needs to be said); it is actually anti-Christian (teaching what is contrary to the Christian faith).

Many reading this will agree but will still wonder if we have to mention God's grace each time we urge Christian obedience. The argument can be made that grace is assumed—people hear it so often that it is the background and foundation for our instruction, even if we don't mention it directly. I cannot categorically deny this possibility but point out that it is hardly the way most people function.

The Human Reflex

Even when we preach grace, most people hear law. They believe that God loves, accepts, and favors them because they have met his requirements. They will acknowledge they are not perfect but believe that God accepts them because they have measured up to some arbitrary standard of goodness. In doing so, they gauge their sufficiency not only by human comparisons ("I am better than most people, or at least better than the worst people") but also by demeaning the holiness of God. They do not recognize that works simply piled up to please God actually further distance us from him; they fall short of his standard of holiness if they are not cleansed by his grace (Isa. 53:6; Luke 17:10).

If grace lies in the mental background of most of those we teach, that is the exception rather than the norm. The human reflex since the fall of our first parents is self-justification: "I qualify for God's benefits because I am good enough." So if all we regularly teach from the Bible is good behavior, we pander to this reflex and deepen its roots in others' hearts. Mature Christian teaching recognizes this innate human way of thinking and resolutely counters it with a regular regimen of grace. Apart from such a diet, anti-Christian reflexes become more entrenched even as we are teaching others to be good.

Mosque or Synagogue Acceptable?

One way of testing whether we are offering a diet of grace sufficient to nurture humble, grateful, and loyal believers is to ask, "Would the message I just taught from God's Word be acceptable in a synagogue or mosque?" Obviously no Jew would be offended by the message "Do not steal." And no Muslim would object to the command "Be faithful to your spouse." But are we really ready for the benediction after we have explored all the dimensions of theft and adultery, and ended with a resounding "Don't do that!"?

Some may honestly answer, "Yes. I believe that my listeners know enough about Scripture that they do not need me to ground all its imperatives in grace this week." Very well. That argument can logically be made. But another question needs to be asked: "Would the message last week also have been acceptable in a synagogue or mosque? And what about the week before that? And the week before that?" If we examine these questions with rigor and honesty and the answer is yes, it's unlikely that listeners have an adequate understanding of grace-motivated and grace-enabled living. And the distinctiveness of the Christian message is almost undeniably lost.

Honoring Savior and Spirit

Being good is important, but teaching (or implying) that people can be good enough to qualify for a holy God's acceptance can only create the dynamics of pride or despair mentioned above (see also chap. 6). Striving for godliness in response to God's grace pleases our Savior. Trying to be good enough for his acceptance apart from his grace insults him. By such striving we imply that his sacrifice in our behalf is irrelevant, and that the empowering of his Holy Spirit in our hearts is unnecessary. We may not intend it, but trying to be good without dependence upon God's grace distances us from him. Our goodness, rather than honoring him, becomes a barrier to the humility by which his blessings enter our lives.

"Be Disciplined"

The last Deadly "Be," "be disciplined," may be the most common in our teaching and preaching because of dynamics previously mentioned. Anyone who regularly teaches the Bible discovers fairly soon that little we say in the way of moral instruction is actually news to most people.

Only Try Harder

Even though people will acknowledge that they fail on many fronts to honor God's requirements, the standards do not surprise them. Hardly anyone walks away from regular exposure to biblical teaching saying, "You're kidding! God really doesn't want me to steal?"

Or, "I never knew the Bible wanted me to be faithful to my spouse [or to forgive people or to control my anger]." Most people sit before our teaching already knowing the biblical imperatives we tell them.

Aware of this, those of us who regularly teach from Scripture spend more time explaining means for fulfilling biblical obligations than introducing people to standards they don't know. Instead of telling them new things to do, we tell them to do what they already know to do, but to do it better than they have before. With variations of urgency, incentive, inspiration, or consequence, we tell people to increase their efforts and to be more consistent in their applications of Scripture.

Just Do More

And to help them get better and better in what they already know to do, we encourage our people to become increasingly disciplined in their spiritual habits. We say, "Read your Bible more. Pray more. Go to church more—especially go to my church more!" Of course, there is nothing wrong with telling people to improve their spiritual disciplines—unless that's all you say.

How do you measure the "more" requirement? How much more will be enough to make a holy God happy or to attain sufficient levels of spiritual development to please him? The answer, of course, is that there will never be enough "more" in our performance to qualify us for God's approval or to insulate us from his judgment. As previously mentioned (see chap. 9), we must learn to see our spiritual disciplines as gracious nourishment rather than heavenly bribes in order for them to bring health into our spiritual lives. But this perspective becomes almost impossible if the message we hear (or say) is only that we must do more, and more, and more.

Grace Magnets Intended

A "more" message—in isolation from the truths of grace that assure us of God's love and make us long for communion with him through his Word, in prayer, and among his people—only trains us to build and maintain our relationship with God on the foundation of our efforts. When the beauty of God's grace magnetizes us to his Word, lifts our hearts in prayer, and binds us to his people in Word, worship, and sacrament, then the spiritual disciplines bless as God intends.

15

How to Balance Grace and Law

Warnings about Deadly "Be" messages do not imply that any such instruction is irrelevant, unimportant, or unnecessary. The Bible clearly gives us examples of people to "be like," many instructions to "be good," and clear guidance to "be disciplined" in exercising the means of grace. So, in light of my strong cautions about forms of the Deadly "Be"—which isolate commands from the grace that should motivate and empower them—I need to reaffirm that I am not suggesting that we ignore or downplay any biblical command. As mentioned earlier, commands to "be" are not wrong *in* themselves; they are wrong *by* themselves.

A Gracious Path

Here's why the commands, despite the distortion of Deadly "Be" teaching, remain important. The law of God is a reflection of his character and care (see chap. 6). He has designed a good and safe path for his people through the instructions of his Word. To deny people understanding of such a path is not at all gracious. Instead, we are obligated by our love for God and his people to be very strong and clear in communicating the path of safety and blessing he has designed for their lives.

We also need to warn people that leaving the path not only dishonors the One who gave it but also endangers the ones who leave it. Yet, even as we warn, we need to make clear that the path has been laid by a hand whose goodness and love have already been proved by his grace—grace that designed the path and grace that restores those who fall from it. Walking the path allows us to experience God's grace, not to earn it. Grace was present when God designed the path and is not simply the destination gained by those who manage to stay on it.

A Clear Goal

By citing the goodness and importance of God's law, I am not now retreating from the need to build such messages on a foundation of grace. Finding just the right balance of law and grace is *not* the goal. Solid biblical teaching is not some midway point on the legalism–license continuum.

In its essence, legalism teaches that we are made right with God by what we do (or don't do): be good, stay pure, go to church a lot, don't lie, don't steal, don't see bad movies, don't cheat—on your spouse or on tests—read your Bible every day, and so on. The essential message is that good behavior gets us to God.

A religious liberal, not nearly so concerned about conservative morality, may seem to teach something very different: care for the poor, clean up the environment, don't tolerate intolerance, love without barriers, provide health care for all, and so forth. But to the extent that people believe these activities will make them acceptable to God, they buy into the same religion as the legalists: good behavior gets us to God. The legalists and liberals differ on what behaviors are best, but not on the premise that our behaviors are our bridge to God.

Never a Balance

Christianity is never a balance between these competing moral-political perspectives. Christianity cannot be found on any spectrum of beliefs where our behavior is the basis of our relationship with God. The Bible teaches that our relationship with God is established by faith in what Jesus Christ has done. His grace alone, not our goodness at all, is what establishes God's love for us.

Whenever our Bible lessons on morality or good behavior leave out that grace, we create confusion, if not contradiction, of the Christian message. That means that those who teach God's Word are not supposed to find a balance between grace and law to lead God's people to a right relationship with him—a little law one week, a little grace the next week, and hope every week that people won't lean too much one way or the other. The gospel is not a balance between law and grace. It is the good news of grace that results in grateful lives of godliness.

Grace, the Foundation and Fuel

Such lives require that we make plain the safe and good path designed by God's instructions in the Bible. But we must make equally plain the reason it remains safe, even when we struggle to stay on it. God's grace designed the path, underlies the path, surrounds its edges, and lies at its end. Those who walk the path without that knowledge know neither the safety nor the peace God intends for their journey with him. Grace should not be balanced with the Bible's commands; it is the foundation for their existence and the fuel for their performance. How we put all that together in our regular application of Scripture is the next question we need to answer.

16

How to Apply Grace to Instruction (Part 1)

When we apply the duties and doctrines of Scripture, we are not simply making sure that we balance proper measures of law and grace; we are building obligation on gratitude.

It's All Organic

Either duty and thanksgiving will be organically related and intrinsically interwoven, or else they will appear to be in tension to one another. Law will appear to be legalism, and grace will appear to be license, unless we build our obedience on the foundation of love generated by grace. Love for God will constrain hearts to lift hands in godly praise in the way we worship, work, and love others.

Four Key Questions

We maintain the organic union of grace and obedience when we consistently answer all four of these questions in our applications of biblical texts: *what, where, why,* and *how.* We'll examine *what* and *where* in this chapter, and *why* and *how* in the next.

What to Do

The *what* question causes us to consider what God requires his people to do as a consequence of the instruction in the biblical text. Sometimes we think of this as the duty the text requires. It may be specifically stated as a command or may be logically derived as an implication of the truth evident in the passage.

Stating what God requires is not legalistic. As mentioned earlier (chap. 6), identifying the path of safety and blessing that God has designed for his people is not ungracious. We help God's people to know the path because walking in God's way honors him, displays the character of his holiness and love, and blesses those who thereby are kept from sadness and suffering they'd experience outside the boundaries of his path.

Once God's people understand that the duty and doctrine in Scripture are intended to promote God's glory and their good, they delight in God's law and want to know its features (Ps. 119:97). They want to honor the God who has saved them by the sacrifice of his Son, and they want to experience the blessings he promises by walking in his ways.

We do no one any favor by withholding the commands of Scripture under some misguided notion that the commands themselves are legalistic. While teaching (or implying) that obedience can merit grace is certainly unbiblical and damaging, not teaching what God commands is equally unbiblical and uncaring. Those whose hearts have been captured by grace want to know how they can serve and please their Savior.

Where to Do It

The duty and doctrine Scripture teaches will not help most people very much if seen as abstract concepts hanging between heaven and earth. If the duty and doctrine we teach seem to have no connection to everyday life, then the God who gave them will seem equally remote. It may be much simpler (and safer) for the Bible teacher to keep from applying the instructions of Scripture to the specific life situations listeners are facing, but that is not what God's people really need or want.

When many of us begin to teach the Bible, we mistakenly believe that God's people don't really want to be challenged by his Word. Yet, while it is certainly true that cold or rebellious hearts do not want God's commands, those whose hearts are warm and sensitive to his Spirit want to hear how they may honor their Lord. They desire to know where the Word of God will make a difference in their lives. They want to be challenged with the Word so that they may walk more closely with the One who gave it.

The specifics desired. Good application identifies how the specific instructions of the Word apply to the specific situations of our lives. Identifying situational specifics for different listeners may appear to be a daunting task. After all, the instructional specifics of application are supplied by the details of the biblical text. But the situational specifics to which these instructions apply usually must come from the life experience of the teacher. The teacher needs to know where listeners are facing spiritual challenges in their lives in order to make helpful and realistic applications.

Two processes will help Bible teachers make such telling applications: (1) do life with God's people; and (2) ask their questions.

What does it mean to "Do life with God's people"? The apostle Paul explained this when he spoke of ministry that made a difference to those at Thessalonica. He said, "We were ready to share with you not only the gospel of God but also our own selves, because you had become very dear to us" (1 Thess. 2:8). When we share our lives with God's people, we have knowledge of their lives that enables us to bring the gospel to the sensitive areas of their situations. Applying the truths of the Scripture is a matter not simply of commentary study but also of rejoicing with those who rejoice and weeping with those who weep (Rom. 12:15)—at graduations and soccer games, in hospitals and homes, at weddings and funerals, at the office and on the hiking trail, at their homes and in yours. It's doing life with God's people.

The questions to ask. When we know their situations, we are able to say where in their lives particular instructions of Scripture should apply. If doing this seems hard, a simple process can help us get beyond abstract application: we can answer the *where* questions by entering the *who* door. After we have discerned the duty or doctrine a passage of Scripture teaches, we open the mental door of our experience with others and ask ourselves, "Who needs to hear this?"

Tact and sensitivity dictate that we rarely identify publicly whom we are addressing (or situational details that would identify them). Instead, we will speak generally about situations such persons are facing rather than the specific people in those situations. This process allows us to speak of categories of persons and say where Scripture applies to them. This way we are able to speak with great sensitivity and specificity to the situations our listeners are facing without identifying specifically who helped us consider those applications.

With this Spirit-aided discretion and insight, people will leave our instruction voicing thankful expressions like "How did you know to say what would be so helpful to me. Have you been reading my mail?" Hopefully, we will not then confess to reading their mail. Instead, we will silently thank the Holy Spirit for bringing to our minds those *who* were struggling in that aspect of life, so that we could direct the truth of the text to *where* it was needed.

Lifting burdens, not making lists. The all-too-common version of scriptural application that compiles lists of duties at the end of a Bible lesson merely burdens people. Application becomes a task of dreaming up new duties that demonstrate the creativity or seriousness of the teacher at the expense of the peace or joy of the listeners. A better approach focuses the duty and doctrine of the text on the actual situations that challenge listeners. Helping them face their challenges with scriptural knowledge and clarity lifts burdens rather than adding weight to concerns they already carry.

Abstract duty and doctrine are easily dodged, and the God who appears to give them is easily marginalized. Lists of duties burden and create resentment of the God who appears only to be a taskmaster. Application that helps people deal with the specific spiritual challenges of everyday life creates appreciation for God's Word and the Shepherd's heart that gave it. That appreciation is necessary to create proper motivation and enabling for Christian living—which are the subjects of the next chapter.

17

How to Apply Grace to Instruction (Part 2)

In the previous chapter we considered the first two of the four key questions that must always be answered to apply biblical instructions: (1) *what* to do; and (2) *where* to do it. This chapter deals with the remaining two key questions that help us apply biblical truth with godly motivation and power: (3) *why* we do what God instructs, and (4) *how* to do what God instructs.

Why We Do It

Telling someone *what* to do and *where* to do it might seem to cover scriptural application, but there is more. If our intention is to build obligation on gratitude, then we also have to make sure that God's people serve him out of appropriate motivations. Along with knowing what to do, we need to know *why* to do it.

Wrong Reasons

As the saying goes, "The right things for the wrong reasons are wrong." That may seem obvious, but without that principle in place we will mislead God's people—even when we give them correct instructions.

How could correct instructions mislead God's people? Think of times in the Old Testament when God told his people that their sacrifices were a stench in his nose (Ps. 51:17; Prov. 15:8; Isa. 65:5; Amos 5:21–22). Sacrifices are actually a good thing and were commanded by God in the Old Testament. But if they were offered simply to placate God so that his people could ignore their sin, or to make sure that Jehovah got his payment so that he would be as nice as the other gods worshiped, then God disdained the sacrifices.

Similarly, if the motivation of our worship today is to placate God so that we can continue in sin, then the worship is sin no matter how correct the wording of our prayers or how enthusiastic our singing. And if the reason that we read our Bibles, lengthen our prayer times, join a church, or act nice is to bribe God to be nice to us, then our spiritual disciplines distance us from his grace rather than earn it.

Honoring Reasons

Motivation is as important as instruction for obedience that truly pleases God. Here's where grace is not only important but integral to application. We need to make sure we have identified the grace of the passage (see chap. 12, and the simplified explanation in chap. 13) in order that our listeners' motivations, as well as their actions, honor God. If we don't, obedience can actually become a barrier to experiencing God's love.

Love for God. By identifying the grace of a passage, we ensure that listeners are not trying to use their obedience to make God love them or merit his acceptance. If God's heart could be bought, our obedience would be bribery, and the degree of his care would be determined by the weight of the "polluted garments" we placed before him (Isa. 64:6).

True obedience is always a loving response to God's grace, rather than a vain attempt to earn it. The heart that comprehends the greatness of God's grace loves him. And love for him compels us to live for him.

Love for those God loves. Love for God also sparks additional loves that please him and motivate his people (see chap. 8). Because we love God, we love whom and what he loves. He loves the unlovely, the outcast, the oppressed, and the orphan and widow in distress. He loves the world he has made and the creatures that inhabit it. As a result, love for God becomes the basis of Christian ethics, stewardship, and mission. Grace will not allow us to settle into a cozy selfishness that ignores a hurting world. A heart captivated by the grace of Christ beats with his concern for his world and all who inhabit it.

Love for the "me" God loves. Love for God also creates an appropriate love for self. It may sound odd and selfish to say that the gospel encourages us to love ourselves, but there is a proper love of "me." We usually discern the need for self-love when we find someone who hates himself or herself. How should we deal with persons who hate their body, bondage, background, appearance, failings, or pain so much that they are doing damage to themselves?

In a generation where anorexia, bulimia, cutting, drug use, and suicide are achingly common, self-hatred must be addressed. How? The Christian response is always some version of saying, "Jesus loves you." That's not wrong. We tell hurting persons that Jesus loves them so that they will learn to treasure themselves. Believers are the temple of the Holy Spirit, the children of Christ's

Father, the creation of his hand, the image of their Lord, and the object of Jesus's sacrificial love—undeniable marks of his love. And if Jesus loves them, then it's okay for them to love themselves—and recognize that their voices of self-hatred are from Satan and not from their Savior.

The grace of Christ, even toward those whose lives have been damaged by their own hand and choices, is the evidence of his love that motivates his children to love themselves to spiritual health. Desiring the blessings of walking with Jesus and avoiding the consequences of sin only make sense if we love ourselves enough to bless our lives with his benefits. The blessings and warnings of Scripture would make no sense (and provide no motivation) for people who had no care for themselves. Loving what and whom he loves—even if the "whom" includes us—is a proper motivation generated by appreciation of Christ's grace toward us.

The Prime Love

What keeps self-love from being selfish? When we love Christ above all, then all loves find their proper order and proportion. Self-love is not improper unless it is our highest love. Jesus explained the priority of our motivations when he said, "You shall love the Lord your God with all your heart and with all your soul and with all your mind. This is the great and first commandment. And a second is like it: You shall love your neighbor as yourself" (Matt. 22:37–39). In this command, love of God, love of others, and love of self are all identified as proper loves by Jesus, but they are also given a proper priority.

The love of God for us that shines through his grace creates a preeminent love for him that enables us to love what and whom he loves, so that we apply his Word to our lives as he intended. Is love the only proper motivation for a Christian? No, but Christ's words about the greatest commandment make it clear that love for God is the foundational motivation of all we do.

We will consider other motivations in the pages to follow. For now, it is enough to recognize that we can make three mistakes in motivating our applications of God's Word. The first is to forget that *proper* motivation is necessary for true obedience. The second is to forget there is a *plurality* of motivations in Scripture: love of God, love of others, and love of self. The third is to forget the *priority* in that order of motivations. We avoid mistaken motivations or priorities by carefully and consistently excavating the grace of every text that generates the love to motivate the obedience God requires.

How to Do It

Knowing *what* to do, *where* to do it, and *why* to do it are necessary elements of biblical obedience. But they are not all that's needed. As previously discussed (see chaps. 7–8), even when specific instructions and good motivations are present, we can still struggle to obey. Passions, distractions, addictions, and rebellion can still derail the progress of the gospel in our lives.

The Change of Heart Required

Everyone who teaches from Scripture hears this question: "I know what God expects, and I want to honor him, but how can I possibly do it?" In other words, the knowledge of what God requires—even combined with the desire to do it—does not guarantee that listeners (or we) will obey. Having knowledge and motivation are necessary, but until we have the power to obey, they are insufficient. How do we do what we know and want to do?

Practical suggestions and encouragements to strive harder are appropriate and helpful—but not sufficient. In addition to knowing what God requires and appealing to the indwelling power of the Holy Spirit through the disciplines of prayer, Bible study, worship, and accountability, we ultimately need a change of heart. The reason is that we will ultimately do what we love the most.

The Change of Heart Provided

Here's where grace plays such a vital role. Because believers are indwelt by the Holy Spirit, we cannot claim that we have no power to resist our sinful impulses. The Bible clearly teaches that Christians are not slaves to sin. We submit to sin when we are drawn away by our own lusts and desires. This really is obvious if we consider that sin would have no appeal and no power in our lives if it did not attract us. We sin when we yield to what tempts us.

So, if the power of sin is our love for it, how do we overcome love for sin? Though I have covered this in earlier chapters (see especially chaps. 7–9), it needs to be repeated here as we are considering why grace is an organic and necessary dimension of biblical application.

We displace love for sin with a greater love. Our wayward loves—which give sin its power in our hearts—are displaced by the love for Christ that is generated by full, regular, sensitive, and powerful exposure to, and explanations of, his grace.

The grace that the Holy Spirit makes integral to every passage of Scripture is there not to enable us to dodge its obligations but to empower them. If we ignore the grace, we unplug the ultimate power of obedience: a supreme love for Christ. To the extent that we expose grace, we endear believers to their Savior, ignite their desire to serve him, and enable their wills to obey him. They will do what he loves most for them to do when they love him most of all.

18

Is Love the Only Biblical Motive?

Is love all there is? I have heard the question enough that I know it needs a little translation: "You keep talking about motivating and enabling Christians with the power of love generated by grace. Are you ever going to talk about any other motivation than this sentimental, schmaltzy, lovey-dovey stuff? After all, does love really have broad enough shoulders and a strong enough backbone to bear the load of Christian obedience in times of crisis, persecution, trial, and crushing temptation? What about the other motivations that appear in the Bible: rewards for obedience, threats of judgment, and, don't forget, 'the fear of the Lord' that is 'the beginning of wisdom.' Is love really all you have to offer for the rigors of obedience in a real world?"

Remember the Plurality and Priority

My answer to the question of how to apply grace (chaps. 16–17) was long, so my related comments here will be a brief reminder. One mistake Christians make about motivation is not recognizing a hierarchy of motivations in the Bible: there is both a *plurality* and a *priority* of motivations.

There are clearly many motivations in the Bible. For example, along with love, our Lord motivates us with blessings for obedience, discipline for disobedience, judgment for unrepentance, hell for the unregenerate, and (I haven't forgotten) "the fear of the Lord" that is "the beginning of wisdom." And these are just a selected few.

So why focus so much on love? Because the Bible's commands tell us of both the plurality *and* the priority of motivations. Love for God is his greatest command, as well as the primary motivation he gives us. All other motivations find their proper order and proportion behind this prime directive (Matt. 22:37–40). As explained more fully in chapters 16–17, love for God is behind proper love for what and whom he loves: his creation and his creatures. We love them because the One we love loves them. That sounds awfully redundant but hopefully makes the point: love for God generates proper regard for what and whom he holds dear.

Rewards and Warnings

Remember also that we are among those he holds dear! We love ourselves (after love of God and others) because he loves us. Such love of self is necessary for the blessings and threats of Scripture to work. If you didn't love yourself, or didn't love God and others above yourself, then the rewards and warnings of Scripture would be either ineffective or counterproductive.

When They Are Spiritually Counterproductive

Promises of blessings or threats of their denial are ineffective motivators for those who have no interest in benefiting or protecting themselves. Rewards and warnings don't work for those with no self-regard.

We should also recognize, however, that rewards and warnings are spiritually counterproductive if we love ourselves above

God or others. In such cases, rewards would feed selfishness. Consequences would be ignored for the same reason. If my primary concern is me, gaining rewards and comforts will take precedence over the life of service and sacrifice to which God calls all believers. In contrast, martyrs have offered themselves to the flames through the centuries not because they had no regard for their lives (they offer to God what he and they hold precious) but because they loved the honor of their Savior above all. Love crowned their motivations and empowered their service and sacrifice.

When They Are Spiritually Helpful

So, if we place love for self in its proper priority behind love for others and love for God, are there other motivations for Christian obedience? The biblical answer is clearly yes. God commands us to believe "he rewards those who seek him" (Heb. 11:6), and "disciplines the one he loves" (Heb. 12:6).

God's positive and negative responses to our behaviors are meant to motivate our obedience. But these motivations produce godliness only within the context of lives that prioritize love for God above love for self.

For example, we need to remember that God's rewards are not always defined by the world's measures and values. "For the kingdom of God is not a matter of eating and drinking but of righteousness and peace and joy in the Holy Spirit" (Rom. 14:17). Only when our greatest delight is fulfilling the purposes of the Lord we love above all do his spiritual rewards make sense or matter at all.

Our Greatest Reward, His Purposes

If we love ourselves, we will desire and pursue the blessings that bring us joy and make us instruments of God's glory. But we should remember that these blessings include the sufferings that allow us to know and claim spiritual rewards beyond the comprehension of those motivated only by material gain or personal comfort (Rom. 5:3–5; Col. 1:24).

When we love God most of all, we are most satisfied when his purposes are most fulfilled in us. We boast in sufferings that promote his glory. We delight in joys that demonstrate his care. We receive without complaint the discipline that conforms us to his likeness and turns us from spiritual harm. We give thanks for the daily bread and special providences that make our lives productive, pleasant, and peaceful. We willingly sacrifice for the sake of magnifying his name. All of these are possible because we love ourselves while loving our God even more than our own lives.

When we love God above all, fulfillment of his purposes is our greatest reward. This reality should make us treasure one last aspect of the categories of biblical motivation. Already we have seen that there are a *plurality* and a *priority* of biblical motivations. Now we should also see how *permeable* those categories are.

Our Greatest Pleasure, His Priority

Because we love God, pleasing him above all pleases us more than anything. Love of God and love of self are not motivations fenced from each other. When we please the One we love the most, we find our own greatest pleasure. Satisfying the One we love most deeply will satisfy us most deeply. Ultimately the Bible motivates us to serve God not out of belabored and begrudging selflessness but out of self-fulfilling joy and satisfaction.

When love for God is our heart's highest priority, then honoring him is our life's greatest joy. Honoring his commands and his calling on our lives is not drudgery but delight when his glory is our highest goal. Selfless service is simultaneously self-satisfaction. Our Savior's concern for our heart's fulfillment, as well as God's glory, underlies the Bible's priority of love for him. Loving our God most is ultimately how we love ourselves best.

19

What about Fear?

The Bible makes it unmistakable that "the fear of the Lord" should motivate God's people to honor him (e.g., Deut. 6:24; Ps. 111:10; Prov. 1:7; Phil. 2:12). No list of biblical motivations is complete without it.

We need to be careful, however, that we do not define biblical fear in ways that contradict what God tells us about the priority or plurality of biblical motivations (see chap. 18). So, what is "biblical" fear?

Biblical Fear

Many references to fearing God occur in the Old Testament, but the New Testament narrative of the birth of Jesus tells us that our Lord comes to enable us to "serve him without fear" (Luke 1:74). The angels told the shepherds, "Fear not," at the Lord's appearing (Luke 2:10). And the apostle John says to those who have been commanded to love God above all, "There is no fear in love, but perfect love casts out fear" (1 John 4:18).

If we are not careful, we could fall into the old error of identifying the God of the Old Testament as the "mean" one, who needs to be feared, and the God of the New Testament as the "nice" one, who wants to be loved. Such a conclusion would have to ignore many verses in each testament that identify our Lord as the one who should be loved *and* feared. So we have to determine how these commands coexist without contradiction in Scripture.

Is Trembling Excluded?

One way we traditionally deal with the tension is to define "fear" with more compatible terms. We realize that there is no good English equivalent for the Hebrew word, so we translate the Hebrew word as "reverence" or "awe." We confess that these terms are not completely equivalent, but we feel they help.

One reason that these substitute terms are not quite adequate is that we can sense what would happen if God were to appear before us in all his glory. We would be like the Israelites at Mount Sinai, or the shepherds when the angels announced Christ's birth. We would tremble in fear. God's mighty power and overwhelming presence would create an understandable caution, apprehension, or awe. If we know what it is to tremble in the presence of a great leader, military power, or natural wonder, then we have some sense of why the Almighty's appearance in shining glory and peals of thunder would cause that kind of fear.

Is Fear of Harm Right?

But what is the nature of the fear that God actually desires? Why does God allow Moses to approach him in behalf of the terrified people, and why do the angels tell the shepherds not to fear? God certainly wants their reverence, and they should remain in awe of him. But the proper fear that honors God is not terror that he is going to harm us. It's more about respect for his holiness, power, and love.

Never fear harm. An old preachers' story tells of a feverish child taken to the doctor. The doctor quickly discerns that an injection is needed. To calm the fears of the child, his mother says, "Johnny, the shot won't hurt." Well, the doctor knows that it will hurt. He also knows that he will probably need the child to trust him for future treatments. So the doctor speaks honestly: "Johnny, I may hurt you, but I will not harm you."

God speaks as honestly to us in his Word. The power and willingness of God to hurt through discipline that steers our lives in holy directions cannot be denied in Scripture. But what we should also realize is that God will never harm his children. Those who are united to Christ are as precious to the Father as his own Son. For them, God's actions are entirely loving, healing, and maturing. He will never harm his own, but will only provide for their ultimate good.

Though God never intends to harm us, this does not deny that discipline may hurt—a lot. The Bible says, "For the moment all discipline seems painful rather than pleasant." But the reason for the discipline is clear: "It yields the peaceful fruit of righteousness to those who have been trained by it" (Heb. 12:11).

God's discipline is never destructive or punitive. The purposes of a heavenly Father's discipline are to turn us from sin's dangers and toward his embrace. That's why the Bible says, "The Lord disciplines the one he loves, and chastises every son whom he receives" (Heb. 12:6). If he did not love us, he would not warn us of sin's consequences or retrieve us from sin's clutches.

Never fear punishment. It may surprise some to read that God's discipline is never punitive. But we need to say this very clearly: believers need never fear punishment from their Father's hand. This does *not* mean that God doesn't care about our sin or won't act to turn us from it. He never punishes his children because punishment involves the imposition of a penalty. And we need to remember that the penalty for all our past, present, and future sin was put on Jesus Christ (Col. 2:13–14; 1 Pet. 2:24; 3:18).

There is now no condemnation or punishment remaining for those who are God's children (Rom. 8:1). But there *is* discipline for God's children. Discipline has an entirely different purpose than punishment. Punishment intends to inflict harm on the guilty in order to impose a deserved penalty for wrongdoing. Discipline intends to turn a person from harm, to restore, and to mature. Both punishment and discipline hurt, but only punishment harms. Discipline helps God's children find peace and the fruits of righteousness.

Perfect Love

If God were to punish us, the fear of terror would be appropriate. But the apostle John writes that perfect love for God casts out that kind of fear precisely because such "fear has to do with punishment, and whoever fears has not been perfected in love" (1 John 4:18). If our obedience is only an attempt to placate or avoid the "ogre in the sky" who is waiting for us to step out of line so that he can punish us, then we haven't understood biblical fear or loved God as he intends.

Excluding Terror

The fear of God that matures us and binds our hearts to his is not the terror that makes us cower and hide. It is actually impossible for us to fulfill God's greatest commandment (to love him with all our heart, soul, strength, and might) if we live in terror of him. The human heart simply cannot respond healthily to the command "Love me or I will do you harm." We may grudgingly serve and obey one who gives such a command, but we cannot love him as Scripture requires. Love is God's greatest command because it provides the willingness and ability to do all that God requires. Biblical fear does not compromise that kind of love.

Exhibited in Christ

Perhaps the best way to understand biblical fear is to remember who best exhibited it. The messianic prophecies of the Old Testament book of Isaiah assure readers of both Christ's coming (11:1) and his character (11:2–4). In describing his character, Isaiah says that Jesus will come in a "Spirit of knowledge and fear of the LORD" and "his delight shall be in the fear of the LORD." The One who knows God best will delight to fear him. The words don't make sense if fear only means cowering in terror. No one would delight in that.

We should interpret the words in light of what we know about the relationship of Jesus and his heavenly Father. Within the heavenly family there can only be perfect love. That love is based upon perfect knowledge of who God is. Such knowledge is not simply awareness of his power, holiness, and wrath toward evil; it includes knowledge of his mercy, tenderness, and love. To delight in proper "fear" of all those is to have a proper regard for the totality of who God is.

Proper Regard

Biblical fear is not simply cowering before God's power and majesty or bowing before his love and mercy. It is a proper regard for all that we know about God's character and care. When we take all of his attributes and actions into our mind's consideration and our heart's commitments, then his worship is our greatest delight. Such fear is not the antithesis of biblical love, but its source.

20

What about Hell?

If it is impossible to express healthy love for someone who threatens, "Love me or I will do you harm," then what's the reason for hell? Doesn't God threaten us with hell so that we will turn to him for our salvation from it? These are great, though hard, questions we must answer.

Why You Can't Scare People into Heaven

Jesus taught that whoever is forgiven much, loves much; and whoever is forgiven little, loves little (Luke 7:47). Love of God—his greatest and foundational commandment—requires that we understand he has forgiven us much. Our love necessitates treasuring his grace, not simply avoiding his wrath. So it remains true that threatening to harm people if they don't love you cannot generate biblical love. Such threats can generate a parody of the obedience God requires, but they cannot generate the love he requires.

This means we can't scare people into heaven. Our union with Christ is not simply a self-serving choice to walk streets of gold rather than be cast into a lake of fire. There is a love of heaven and a fear of hell that are straight from Satan if they are only about self-serving interests. In order for us to experience the joys heaven intends for the relationship Christ has secured for us, we must love him. The love that pleases God and satisfies us is not and cannot entirely be a product of trying to keep an ogre in the sky off our backs.

Justice and Mercy Required

In order for hell to motivate biblical obedience and love, it must represent more than the pique of a frowning deity who has been crossed. To motivate genuine holiness, hell must first be perceived as the just destiny of those who have broken the righteous standards of God. Those standards must also be seen as rooted in the holiness of God, and their transgression as deserving an eternal penalty. When all this is understood, then the *mercy* of God that saves us from the just penalty of hell, more than hell itself, is what generates love for him. Knowledge that we are forgiven much causes us to love much—heaven's basic requirement (Matt. 22:37–38).

Rescue from Life Desired

But here's the problem: this very mature understanding of the righteousness, justice, and mercy of God is not where most people begin their Christian walk. Most people turn to Christ because they have despaired of this life, not because they are dodging a hellish afterlife. If escaping God's judgment is all that motivates, then most are unlikely to love him as he requires.

Most persons' initial love for Christ stems from his rescue from the present "hell" of their earthly existence: loneliness, emptiness, guilt, shame, depression, slavery to addiction, relational trauma, and so on. That is why Jesus was being true to the human experience as well as his spiritual task when he said, "Come to me, all who labor and are heavy laden, and I will give you rest" (Matt. 11:28). He understood that the pains of this life could be as compelling as the threats of the next.

Making Sense of Eternal Punishment

I cannot deny that there are some who seek Christ's mercy because they believe that they have committed sins worthy of an eternal hell. This is undeniable in a world of mass murder, child abuse, genocide, ethnic cleansing, rape, jihad, and systematic torture. We should praise God when souls awaken to the evil of such crimes and see them for the hell-deserving sins they are.

A Common Misunderstanding

But such an awakening is not where most people are intellectually or spiritually when they first turn to the Savior. Early in their Christian experience most people have no concept of what they have done that would deserve eternity in hell. Even if they echo thoughts they have heard from a pulpit, or feel deep and profound guilt, few could identify why they would deserve an eternal hell of suffering for their sin.

Theologians frequently defend the doctrine of hell with the rationale that people are deserving of the infinite and eternal torments of hell because sin is against an infinitely holy and eternal God. That may make sense to a theologian, but it will not ring true or fair to almost anyone else.

If even Hitler, Genghis Kahn, or Idi Amin were to scream in agony for ten thousand years in a lake of fire, most persons (especially believers, who are made in God's image and weigh what is just according to the standards and heart he grants) would be ready to end these monsters' pain. And arguing that such an unending hell of physical torment awaits the Jewish, Hindu, or nominal

Christian grandmother whose greatest earthly crime appears to be a sharp tongue, seems outside any standard of justice that we associate with Christ's nature.

Christ's Intention

So, how do we explain why Jesus spoke about hell more than anyone else in the Bible? At least a partial answer lies in understanding that Jesus reserved his harshest words for those who were relying on their self-righteousness to gain them heaven. They needed to know that total, conscious, eternal separation from the blessings of God (that's a pretty good summary of the Bible's teaching on hell, taking into account all its discussions and metaphors, such as the eternal lake of fire, maggots, torturers, darkness, gnashing of teeth, and whippings) was the future of all who did not seek God through his Son.

Jesus's greatest expressions of mercy and grace were poured out on those who believed they had no hope of heaven due to their background, failings, and sin. Their despair of God's care in this life, and of his provision of spiritual security for the next life, made Christ's grace welcome and powerful. His love for the unlovely, the outcast, and the despicable is what drew hearts to him. He usually spoke of hell only with the intention of making the proud understand how desperate they were apart from him. The self-righteous, no less than the obvious sinners, needed to long for his grace in order for heaven to be their eternal destiny.

The Hell of Earth and Eternity

If simply scaring people with hell's threats will not move them to love the God of heaven as he requires, why is hell so prominent in the Bible? Surely part of the answer is to help people turn from the hell *on earth* that results from relying on their own wisdom and ways for peace and satisfaction. The hell of their creation here is the hell of their captivity in eternity.

Getting What You Want

One reason that hell is eternal is that no one there says to God, "Let me out—I want to honor and serve you now!" Hell is total, conscious, *eternal* separation from the blessings of God because the eternal souls there get exactly what they want: total and continuing autonomy from his gracious influence and care.

For believers (those for whom Scripture is primarily written, and for whose motivation its metaphors are designed), such autonomy from their Savior would be agony. Christ's warning them of hell and offering to save them from its just consequences is a grace that makes them want him forever. For those who desire self-rule and selfishness more than the Savior, hell is also getting what they want forever: the absence of God's benevolence. C. S. Lewis neatly summarizes this spiritual dynamic by saying, "The doors of hell are locked on the inside,"[1] because the sinful always love darkness instead of light (John 3:19).

Though the sinful suffer in hell, they prefer its agonies to honoring Christ's glory. Perhaps this is because, as John Piper writes, "God rejecters might be as miserable in heaven as in hell."[2]

Giving the Grace of Warning

Christ speaks so much about hell because his grace requires that he warn all of the consequences of their choices. Because God is holy and just, he will vindicate his honor, purify his kingdom, and punish wickedness. Grace requires that he do each of these. His

---

1. C. S. Lewis, *The Problem of Pain* (New York: Macmillan, 1962), 128.
2. John Piper, *The Romantic Rationalist: God, Life, and Imagination in the Work of C. S. Lewis* (Wheaton, IL: Crossway, 2014), 152.

grace also compels him to offer peace to those alarmed by the realities of hell. An old American hymn still rightly instructs us:

> Praise the grace whose threats alarmed thee,
>   Roused thee from thy fatal ease;
> Praise the grace whose promise warmed thee,
>   Praise the grace that whispers peace.[3]

For those who turn from Christ's grace, God maintains his holiness and exercises his justice by allowing unbelievers to feast on the fruits of their own decisions. They will lie in the bed of their own making, experiencing the hell of isolation from God's gracious kingdom that they forever choose. But for those who turn to Christ's grace, God accomplishes all that his justice and holiness require through the life, sacrifice, and victory of his Son, so that those who believe may rest eternally in his love.

The message of hell is *not* opposed to the grace of God. We can teach it in ungracious ways if we try to scare people into heaven without connecting the dots of justice and mercy that cause love for him to triumph over terror of him. If we never warn of eternal consequences, we fail to exercise Christ's grace. But if we do not speak of the grace that rescues people from the hell of their own creation on earth as well as the hell of God's design and deprivation in eternity, we make it difficult for them to love him as his Word requires and his heart desires.

---

3. Francis Scott Key, "Lord with Glowing Heart I'd Praise Thee," 1817.

21

Does Sin Change Anything?

Encouraging obedience through the heart chemistry of grace and through gracious warnings of sin's consequences can create obvious tensions. Heart chemistry requires that people be assured of God's love, mercy, and forgiveness. Warnings require that people be made aware of consequences, discipline, and judgment. How do we fit these together without risking the loss of God's affection? Can nothing really change in our relationship with God, even if our sin betrays him?

Conditional Relationships

The conditional nature of many human relationships accustoms us to thinking that God's love will increase or decrease with the degree of our obedience. If our own parents, coaches, or employers have made our acceptance depend on our accomplishment, then we can get into the habit of thinking of life as a basketball game: score enough points, and you gain acceptance and acclaim; mess up, and you are relegated to the far end of the bench.

Plain talk about the consequences of sin may reinforce this

misconception. Sin in a believer's life may well result in spiritual discipline and painful consequences. Sin in an unbeliever's life will certainly have earthly and eternal consequences. But these truths do not indicate that God alters his affection because his children sin.

Parental Parallels

When my children disobey, I may get angry, impose discipline, and allow consequences in order to train them in life patterns I know will be better for them. I am an imperfect parent, so I mess up by not always doing these selflessly and with my children's welfare as my first priority. Yet, no matter how bad their disobedience, they are still my children. That relationship does not change, even though my attitude and actions toward them may change.

As a perfect parent, our heavenly Father measures all these dynamics perfectly and graciously. He may also be angry, impose discipline, and allow consequences in order to train us in life patterns that will bless our lives. His grace makes our good his priority in every divine action.

He doesn't mess up. Without sacrificing one iota of his glory, he perfectly balances every measure of mercy and consequence. Though his actions and approval may vary, our relationship with him does not. The grace that removes our guilt from us also secures his love for us, which never alters. We remain his children, secure in the love that motivates and enables renewed obedience.

What Does and Doesn't Change

To get the balance right in our responses to God, consider what can and what cannot change in our relationship with him (see table 1). This list does not exhaust all the aspects of our relationship with God that can and cannot change. My hope is that the list is long

Table 1. Our relationship with God[a]

WHAT CAN CHANGE	WHAT CANNOT CHANGE
Our fellowship[b]	Our family status[c]
Our experience of his blessing[d]	His desire for our welfare
Our assurance of his love[e]	His affection for us
His delight in our actions[f]	His love for us
His discipline	Our destiny[g]
Our feelings of guilt	Our freedom from condemnation[h]

a. See Bryan Chapell, *Holiness by Grace: Delighting in the Joy That Is Our Strength* (Wheaton, IL: Crossway, 2001), 196.

b. By "fellowship" I mean the day-to-day sense of enjoyment we have in communing with God and knowing his approval of our actions. For a more technical discussion of the term and its conditional nature, see John Murray, *The Covenant of Grace* (1953; repr., Phillipsburg, NJ: Presbyterian and Reformed, 1988), 19; also, John Murray, *Principles of Conduct* (Grand Rapids, MI: Eerdmans, 1957), 198.

c. Rom. 8:15; 1 John 3:1.

d. God never ceases to bless his people in the sense of working all things together for their good (Rom. 8:28). Even his discipline intends to turn them from harm and toward the Savior (Heb. 12:11). However, our experience of his chastening love versus his approving love is very different.

e. See the Westminster Confession of Faith, 18.4: "True believers may have the assurance of their salvation divers ways shaken, diminished, and intermitted; as, by negligence in preserving of it, by falling into some special sin which woundeth the conscience and grieveth the Spirit; by some sudden or vehement temptation, by God's withdrawing the light of His countenance, and suffering even such as fear Him to walk in darkness and to have no light: yet are they never utterly destitute of that seed of God, and life of faith, that love of Christ and the brethren, that sincerity of heart, and conscience of duty, out of which, by the operation of the Spirit, this assurance may, in due time, be revived; and by the which, in the mean time, they are supported from utter despair."

f. God's unconditional and eternal affection for us does not mean that he approves wrongdoing, nor that he will fail to deal with it for our good (Ps. 118:18; Eph. 4:30).

g. John 10:28; Rom. 8:28–30, 35–39. See also Bryan Chapell, *In the Grip of Grace: When You Can't Hang On* (Grand Rapids, MI: Baker, 1992), 91–116.

h. Rom. 8:1. Feelings of guilt are the subjective experience of guilt that we have when we betray Christ's love and grieve the Holy Spirit. God uses them to turn us from sin. However, the objective judgment of our sin has already and forever been placed on Christ's cross so that we will never again bear guilt that separates us from God's heart (Rom. 8:35–39; Gal. 2:20).

enough to explain how God's grace secures our hearts to him, even as he deals graciously with our sin.

Why Assurance Can Change

Still, it may seem odd, in a book detailing how our security in God's grace motivates and enables our obedience, to see (in the middle of the table) that our sin can affect our assurance of his love. But this has to be said: God's assurances of his mercy and pardon apply to those who love him (Rom. 8:28). And nowhere does the Bible define love as presuming upon God's grace and his pardon in order to betray him.

If we persist in sin without remorse or repentance, we have little biblical foundation for claiming that God's grace applies to us (Rom. 6:1–2; Heb. 10:26–27). He may well love us despite our rebellion, but we will have little assurance inside our own hearts (what we feel, not what God alone knows to be real) if rebellion is our habit. Grief for sin, remorse for our betrayal, and sorrow for the harm we have done are all evidences in our hearts of the Holy Spirit's presence (Eph. 4:30; James 4:8–10). If we are not experiencing these, we will have little personal assurance, regardless of God's persevering love for us.

The Assurance of Grief

We could not grieve for sin and would not be concerned about our relationship with God if our hearts had not already been transformed by his grace (Rom. 8:5; 1 Cor. 2:14). Hearts untouched by the Spirit do not desire his presence, but instead hate his ways and are hardened against his love. In a strange but special mercy during our times of doubt, sorrow that we have betrayed and grieved the God who loves us is the assurance of the Spirit in us.

Genuine concern that our sin has removed us from God's care

should cause us to rejoice—such concern is actually evidence of God's care, a sign of spiritual life in us. Such concern is the first step toward biblical repentance that restores our fellowship with God.

The Limits of Repentance

Here it is important to note that the restoration is of *fellowship*—a close and loving daily communion with God—not of *relationship*. Again, it is important to stress that our relationship does not change, even if our repentance for specific sins has not occurred or is not complete. We remain children of God even if we have gone to the far country of spiritual rebellion or apathy (Luke 15:11–32). We may not have personal assurance of that relationship in an unrepentant state, but that does not mean the relationship has dissolved.

Repentance does not determine relationship. Believers' continuing relationship with Christ is not affected by their daily repentance. Here I am *not* referring to the repentance that occurred when we initially confessed our need of Christ. At that time, we hated and confessed our sin, turned from it unto our God, and placed our faith in Christ's work in our behalf, receiving his grace, resolving to follow in his paths, and resting in his provision for now and eternity. At that same moment, God declared us forgiven, cleansed, adopted, and forever united to Christ.

Notice the reality of God's establishment of a family relationship with us at the time of our initial repentance. We are from that moment accounted as his children, clothed with Christ's righteousness, and already seated with him at God's right hand (Eph. 1:13; 2:6; 5:1). That family status is not jeopardized by the flaws and failures of my daily repentance. God is not withholding his grace for sins I do not remember to repent of, do not know to repent of, have recognized but not adequately confessed, have partially recognized but not fully confessed, have confessed but not fully renounced, or have confessed and renounced but then repeated. I do not stop being a child of God because I am a problem child.

Here we must deal with a common way some people have been taught to think about gaining God's forgiveness. Some of us have been led in prayers of daily repentance (asking forgiveness for the faults and weaknesses in our everyday walk with Christ) with the wording of 1 John 1:9: "If we confess our sins, he is faithful and just to forgive us our sins and to cleanse us from all unrighteousness." Since this instruction is true, isn't the flip side of the coin also true—that if we don't confess our sins, God won't forgive our sins? The answer to this question must be a strong *no way!* or we are all in great danger.

I am not at all saying that daily repentance is unnecessary. It is necessary if we are to experience the blessings and fellowship of a heart resonant with Christ's. But daily repentance does not make or break our core relationship with him. Our confession is not about attempting to convince God of our contrition, nor about qualifying for his grace. Rather, biblical confession is a humble seeking after the rest his grace has already provided through Christ. Similarly, repentance is not about earning grace but entering it; not about quenching his wrath but quieting the accusations of our hearts; not about unlocking his mercy but releasing our sin-sick sorrow to the Savior, who already rejoices to receive it. To think otherwise is to go down a dangerous path.

Repentance does not cause forgiveness. If either God's present love or his eternal forgiveness of us is determined by the presence or quality of our repentance, we are all in terrible danger. Because our hearts and understanding are yet imperfect, we remain blind to sins we will see only with further maturity—and perhaps not until eternity (Ps. 19:12).

And if our full forgiveness of the sins we do see requires complete and proper repentance, none of us are fully forgiven. None of us have repented as fully, deeply, or completely as a holy God requires. Does this mean we are not fully forgiven? No. We are dead to our sin and alive in Christ—united to him, hidden in him, and made completely pure by faith in his blood, not by faith in the adequacy of our repentance (Rom. 6:10–11; 1 Pet. 3:18).

The Blessings of Repentance

The more we repent, the more we remove barriers from our fellowship with Christ, and the more we experience the joy of the forgiveness he has already secured for us. Forgiveness is the ocean that already surrounds us when we launch our prayers of repentance to God. We do not manufacture the ocean by our repentance; we sail in the peace its boundless waters provide.

Repentance does not earn our forgiveness; repentance allows us to experience the peace of being forgiven. Those who have trusted in Christ are already, entirely, and forever clothed in his righteousness (Gal. 3:27; Col. 3:4). Our God is now "for us"; his every dealing with us is out of a heart that is tuned "for grace"— that's what *forgiveness* is, the desire *for grace* to bless the soul of another (Rom. 8:32). That means that even when we experience the consequences of our sin under divine discipline, we are no less forgiven. God's intentions are still entirely grace-motivated. He intends and gives only what is best for us and our fellowship with him.

Forgiveness and pardon. But how can we believe that God provides complete forgiveness for past, present, and future faults and, at the same time, expect that God may bring consequences for our sin? The answer is that forgiveness is not the same thing as pardon. Forgiveness is the provision of grace that obliterates relational barriers between us and God. Pardon is the removal of the consequences of sin. Because God forgives, he desires only what is spiritually best for the guilty. Because God desires what is good for us and those whose lives we touch, he may not pardon all the earthly consequences of the sin he has eternally forgiven. This means he may fully forgive the murderer of his sin and still require jail time.

All believers will experience eternal pardon for their sin, but grace now requires that consequences sometimes be allowed in this life to turn us from greater sin and harm (Eph. 4:28; 6:4; 2 Thess. 3:10). God's forgiveness is still present and still cancels our guilt, but pardon of temporal consequences remains subject to his wisdom, mercy, and justice as he weighs what is best for our spiritual and societal good.

Grace, capturing and compelling. Grace is never out of view. Grace secures our relationship with God despite our sin. Grace maintains our forgiveness despite the inadequacies of our repentance. Grace filters the consequences of sin in order to protect us from spiritual harm. When this grace captures our hearts, it compels us to love and serve the God who provides its lavish, loving, and lasting provisions.

Sensitizing us to the lavish, loving, and lasting love of God is ultimately the divine purpose for our daily repentance. As we repent, we are reminded of how great is his love for us, and how great a betrayal of him is our sin. Our repentance does not earn his favor; it expresses our sickness over our own sin and our desire to turn from it into a closer walk with him. As we confess our sin, he is always faithful to forgive our sin. But securing his faithfulness is not our object; securing our faithfulness is.

Too many people cease confessing their sin because they despair of ever ceasing to sin. They figure that God will grow exasperated with their repeated confessions. To such persons we must say,

"Keep on confessing." The Lord will not tire of the weak and weary who come to him. His grace is too great. Rather, if we are faithful in confessing our sin, he is forever faithful to keep forgiving our sin.

In addition, God will use our daily, dogged, and unrelenting confessions to create a growing distaste for our sin so that we have to spit it out of our lives—as mature repentance requires. If we faithfully confess our sin and then sin again, we should not hesitate to confess again, and again, and again—until our souls sicken of whatever is coming between us and the God who never sickens of our coming to him.

Confession is good for the soul, even if we need to do it over and over for the same sin. Repetition of a sin is no reason to abandon confession. He who urged us to forgive seventy-seven times has the heart stamina for many more of our confessions (Matt. 18:22). Our God's patient and persevering grace, regularly appealed to, stimulates love for him and hatred of sin that is the heart chemistry of spiritual victory.

General Index

Scripture Index

To learn more about Unlimited Grace,
the teaching ministry of Bryan Chapell,
please visit **unlimitedgrace.com.**
While there, you can also register to
receive free weekly devotionals and
other online resources.

Also Available from Bryan Chapell

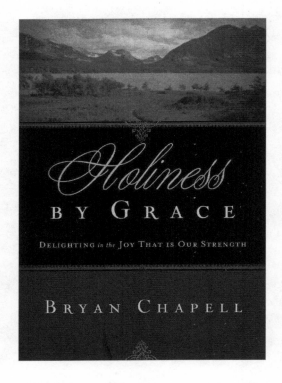

Discover the gracious source of joy and strength
you'll need for a lifelong pursuit of holiness.

For more information, visit crossway.org.